DIMINISHING INDIA

DECADES OF BRAZEN POLITICAL APATHY

B R Taneja
Rakesh Duda

OPUS

OPUS

Published by Vitasta Publishing Pvt Ltd
Vitasta Publishing Pvt Ltd
2/15, Ansari Road, Daryaganj
New Delhi - 110 002
info@vitastapublishing.com

ISBN 978-81-948200-7-9

First Edition 2021

MRP ₹595

Edited by Veena Batra
Cover and Layout by Vit Books
Printed by Chaman Enterprises, New Delhi

Contents

Dedication *v*

Authors' Note *vii*

Prologue *ix*

Legacy of Poverty 1

Indian Police Under Captivity 75

Waiting For Justice—Interminably 97

Diminishing Democracy 138

References *215*

About The Author *225*

Dedicated to
the relentless composure and patience shown for decades by millions of starving, malnourished and sick fellow Indians who live on the hope that things would change for them... someday.

AUTHORS' NOTE

We would like to caution the readers that we have no pretensions of being academicians or researchers. Esoteric and astute analysis should, therefore, not be expected in this book. It reflects on the concerns that we are faced with and these are analysed without getting lost in the web of academic over-analysis. But, we have tried to deal with issues with the level of intellectual honesty and conviction that, ideally, every person belonging to the educated class should have.

We are corporate professionals who spend the working hours analysing plans and performance reports and carrying out mundane business management activities. However, we have a more than hobby level interest in public policy and political economy.

The idea of making an attempt to write this book germinated from the question that is thrown at us every day—why are we a poor nation even after having attained independence seven decades back? We were unable to put together or even get a cogent answer and, hence, decided to take this journey of making an attempt to find an answer and also see if we could propose some solutions.

We are not sure of how the hardcore academicians and researchers would react to our analysis. To build up our arguments, we have relied mainly on macro-level data that is available in the public domain and refrained from micro-analysis lest we lose sight of the woods for the sake of counting the trees. We believe that it is meaningless to work overtime to get, for example, an exact estimate of poverty in the country when we know that it is rampant and we get to see it around us all the time. We realised that by getting obsessively involved and concerned as researchers about establishing the scale and the consequences of the problems that we are faced with, we would lose our capability to look at issues objectively and find effective solutions that are simple, but bold and transformative and require political conviction to implement.

We are sure about the concern we have about the problem and the honesty with which we have put forth our analysis and point of view. Our objective is to motivate people to start thinking about real issues that we are struggling with. We hope to achieve this in a small way but only if the readers react to what we have tried to enumerate. Problems have to be identified and efforts made to accept that these exist. Once that is done, solutions can be found; these are often staring us in the face. We believe in what the American author, Asa Don Brown, had so simply stated, "Problem solving is an everyday occurrence in life".

Please reach out to us with your views, comments, criticism (even praise—if we deserve any) and we shall be happy to engage with you.

—B R Taneja and Rakesh Duda

PROLOGUE

It was a tumultuous ninety-year, violent and non-violent struggle (1857 to 1947) that Indians of diverse sociocultural backgrounds and political ideologies had to undertake across India to generate the realisation in the British administration that they would not be able to hold the Indian sub-continent within its Empire. The British Empire was left with little choice and India had to be declared an independent nation; this happened on 15 August 1947.

Of the existing 1.3 billion of the Indian population, only about 4 million people could have memories of the jubilation that was so palpable on the streets of Delhi and other parts of the country. Most of these people, even with their fading memories of the distant past, would be, nostalgically, remembering how they participated in the celebrations at the end of close to two centuries of subjugation led misery that the people had to go through. Thousands of men and women came out on the streets and *maidaans* cheering, singing and marching in processions with fervour on 14 August. It was a day on which people felt psychologically unshackled and developed a sense of collective responsibility towards nation building. It must have been the most cherished and delightful sight when the Union Jack was lowered at the Viceroy's House for the last time on this day.

At the forefront of this new hope being kindled were Mahatma Gandhi, Jawaharlal Nehru, and Sardar Patel. Gandhi, who was away in Kolkata (then Calcutta) from 9 August 1947 trying to restore communal peace in Bengal, was a hurt and disillusioned man with the creation of Pakistan.[1] On 14 August 1947 he said, "From tomorrow we shall be delivered from the bondage of the British rule. But from midnight today, India will be partitioned too. While, therefore, tomorrow will be a day of rejoicing, it will be a day of sorrow as well. It will throw a heavy burden of responsibility upon us. Let us pray to God that He may give us strength to bear it...."[2]

Nehru was centre-stage and on the stroke of midnight on 14 August the first prime minister of free India addressed the Indian Constituent Assembly; this was broadcast live over All India Radio. In this speech Nehru outlined his vision for India. The Constituent Assembly that was elected and founded on 6 July 1946 with 389 members (these were reduced to 299 after the partition of the country) took close to three years to put the Constitution together. Nehru's midnight speech reflected clearly what independent India ought to be looking forward to as a nation-state. And the Constitution of India that came into existence twenty-nine months after this historic speech was completely supportive of the policies and programmes that were to follow.

Fifty-eight years old Nehru, who had emerged as the tallest leader of the Congress Party and Mahatma's preferred choice for the top job, established that he deserved the job that he was given when he addressed the Constituent Assembly like a seasoned statesman and said:

> *Long years ago we made a tryst with destiny, and now the time comes when we shall redeem our pledge, not wholly or in full measure, but very substantially.*
> *At the stroke of the midnight hour, when the world sleeps, India will awake to life and freedom. A moment comes, which comes but rarely in history, when we step out from the old to the new, when an age ends, and when the soul of a nation, long suppressed, finds utterance.*
> *It is fitting that at this solemn moment we take the pledge of dedication to the service of India and her people and to the still larger cause of humanity....*
> *Freedom and power bring responsibility. The responsibility rests upon this assembly, a sovereign body representing the sovereign people of India. Before the birth of freedom we have endured all the pains of labour and our hearts are heavy with the memory of this sorrow. Some of those pains continue even now. Nevertheless, the past is over and it is the future that beckons to us now.*
> *That future is not one of ease or resting but of incessant striving so that we may fulfil the pledges we have so often taken and the one we shall take today. The service of India means the service of the millions who suffer. It means the ending of poverty and ignorance and disease and inequality of opportunity.*

The ambition of the greatest man of our generation has been to wipe every tear from every eye. That may be beyond us, but as long as there are tears and suffering, so long our work will not be over....

We rejoice in that freedom, even though clouds surround us, and many of our people are sorrow-stricken and difficult problems encompass us. But freedom brings responsibilities and burdens and we have to face them in the spirit of a free and disciplined people....

The future beckons to us. Whither do we go and what shall be our endeavour? To bring freedom and opportunity to the common man, to the peasants and workers of India; to fight and end poverty and ignorance and disease; to build up a prosperous, democratic and progressive nation, and to create social, economic and political institutions which will ensure justice and fullness of life to every man and woman.

We have hard work ahead. There is no resting for any one of us till we redeem our pledge in full, till we make all the people of India what destiny intended them to be. We are citizens of a great country, on the verge of bold advance, and we have to live up to that high standard. All of us, to whatever religion we may belong, are equally the children of India with equal rights, privileges and obligations. We cannot encourage communalism or narrow-mindedness, for no nation can be great whose people are narrow in thought or in action.

To the nations and peoples of the world we send

greetings and pledge ourselves to cooperate with them in furthering peace, freedom and democracy.

And to India, our much-loved motherland, the ancient, the eternal and the ever-new, we pay our reverent homage and we bind ourselves afresh to her service.[3]

This epoch speech is much talked about but never referred to or looked into for understanding what Nehru felt and envisioned. It is considered to be one of the best speeches delivered in the 20th century[4] and, interestingly, he did not read it from a written text. However, ironically, in the last six decades, this speech has acquired the respectful status that is akin to the ritualistic respect that the younger members of a business family show for the garlanded and photo-framed picture of their grandfather for laying the foundations of the business; while no efforts are made to know or understand what the founder believed in and how he achieved what he did. Every statement of the speech clearly reflected his concerns. Since this speech laid the foundation for post-colonial India, it is important to reflect on and evaluate how India has progressed in the last six decades especially in the framework of what was envisioned for her to achieve. Nehru's ambition was to build a prosperous, democratic and progressive nation and to create social, economic and political institutions which would ensure justice and fullness of life to every man and woman and equal rights and privileges for children. His concerns were with peace, poverty, ignorance, disease, and inequality of opportunities.

As a nation we seem to have lost focus of these issues. We have moved away from fundamental issues of poverty alleviation and access to basic human facilities and created a society that thrives on disparity in income and opportunities. In the pages that follow, the authors have attempted to objectively and critically examine how the various governments, in the last six decades, have performed on the objectives articulated at the time of independence by the first prime minister of the country.

It is an established fact that successive governments have taken the poor for granted. In fact, there seems to be a strategic intent to keep people in the state that they are in—uneducated, unemployed, helpless but prone to getting hopeful and swayed in the direction of the party that promises the most every time the quinquennial electoral process is carried out. The poor are largely dependent on the succour available to them through government policies, the protection and the resolution of conflicts that they ought to get from the police, and the justice that should be meted out to them. Ironically, a sizeable percentage of the population of the country is used by the politicians, harassed and exploited by the police and kept at an inaccessible distance, because of its ivory tower status and approach, by the Judiciary. The authors discuss these three issues in some detail and even suggest remedial actions. In addition, the authors have tried to analyse the reasons for our not adopting the Presidential form of government despite it being discussed in the Constituent Assembly of India. Their contention is that if the Presidential form of government was adopted, it could have made a huge difference to our polity and governance.

Legacy of Poverty

In a country well governed, poverty is something to be ashamed of. In a country badly governed, wealth is something to be ashamed of.

—Confucius
(Chinese philosopher)

Unemployment is a great tragedy. The man who goes about hopelessly seeking work in order to earn bread for his children is a living reproach to civilization.

—Carlos Saavedra Lamas
(Argentine academic, politician and Nobel Peace Prize recipient)

AT THE end of the two centuries of British rule the Indian economy was primarily agricultural with some presence in textiles, handicrafts, metal and precious stone industries which had survived the aggressive British onslaught. People in independent India of 1947 were socially and economically deprived, uneducated, unemployed, poor, malnourished, diseased, resourceless and bereft of any hope. A sizeable population of those in the states of Bengal, Punjab, Gujarat, Rajasthan, Delhi and Jammu & Kashmir had the extra burden of having a large population of displaced refugees from the newly created Pakistan. It is estimated that about 0.5 to 2 million[1] people were killed or went missing during partition.

It was probably the most difficult period in the history of contemporary India—fifteen million traumatised people[2] (more than 35 per cent of the population of England in 1947) crossed the borders on either side to restart their lives ab initio. But, all this trauma and agony did not take away the excitement of having attained independence after a ninety-year struggle and two hundred years of ruthless and systematic exploitation by the East India Company and the British Empire. The new-found freedom was psychologically far too engaging to even think of the state of affairs inherited from the British.

In all the turmoil that existed through the first few years after independence—which was all about rehabilitation of refugees and attempts to put together a model of governance that would take care of the needs of the nation and her people—there was an air of hope. Hope stemming from the fact that it would not be the British Crown and its representatives that would decide the fate of Indians. It would be their own leaders, who they had engaged with and supported through the freedom movement, and who they could elect or reject in the first Lok Sabha elections that were to be held in 1951-52. It was ironical that just about twenty thousand British 'masters'[3] were able to exploitatively manage and control close to 390 million people in undivided India.[4] It was not only freedom from the rule of a nation that used to send its people, who had nothing in common with the local population, on a four to six months voyage to take up administrative positions in India but the empowerment and acquisition of the democratic right to elect their own government.

The intellectual and political elite, though divided in different political and ideological camps, had a vision for independent India which was shared over years with the people to garner the momentum for the freedom movement. The entire freedom movement was based on generating the hope that things would change for the better after the British rulers went back. Two years and five months after independence the country got its Constitution, which is considered to be the longest constitution in the world[5] probably for good reasons, as it had to address so many issues. It had to address India's integration as a nation state; assure and comfort the minorities in the aftermath of partition; define a new socioeconomic paradigm that would help uplift millions of people who were poor and deprived; eliminate religious and social discrimination and give the people of the country the right to express their thoughts and beliefs. Seventy years after having attained independence and after having kick-started on such an amazingly progressive note, something has gone very wrong. As a nation we have quadrupled our population to 1380 million[6] from 330 million in 1947[7] but have comprehensively failed to achieve what we had set out to do. In fact, we have added a whole new class of problems that the State needs to address with political will and conviction. These ought to be based on the uncompromising desire to uphold the tenets of the Constitution and not being lured by the sole objective of acquiring or retaining power.

Over the years, the government of India and the various think-tanks in the country that support and engage with it have been working to estimate the extent of poverty in the country. The last report on the definition of 'poverty line' was worked on by an expert committee set up by the then Planning Commission in 2011-2012 under the chairmanship of C Rangarajan, the former Chairperson of Prime Minister's

Economic Advisory Council. According to this report, the new poverty line was Rs 32 per day per person in rural areas and Rs 47 per day per person in urban areas.[8] Earlier corresponding figures recommended by the Tendulkar Committee were Rs 27 for rural and Rs 33 for urban areas.[9]

The Rangarajan Committee was set up against the backdrop of a national outrage over the Planning Commission's suggestion of defining poverty line at Rs 22 per person per day.[10] The Rangarajan Report had put 363 million[11] Indians below the poverty line that it had defined—this incidentally is 30 million more than the population of India at the time of partition. Out of this staggering number, an equally staggering number of approximately 51 million people are estimated to be living in extreme poverty.[12] This is three-fourths of the total population of England or France, one and a half times the population of Canada, and twice the population of Australia.

Notwithstanding how the UN defines poverty and extreme poverty or how the policymakers define the poverty line, the fact remains that in India poverty stares us in the face—with varying degrees of intensity—in all the regions and states. Every fourth Indian is poor and that too as per the definition of a committee that has, somehow, managed to come to the conclusion that people who have access to anything more than Rs 47 per day in an urban area or Rs 32 in a rural area cease to be poor.

These amounts are just enough to keep people off starvation. But, the present day Homo sapiens also need shelter, clothing, medical care, education for children, etc. to survive. If this was to be accepted as the poverty line, then all the 363 million people who are living below the poverty line should live without hope of their, or their progeny, ever being able to cross over to the other side of the line. This definition of poverty line is a sad and dehumanised commentary on the thought process of its authors. The poverty line which segregates the poor from the non-poor should be defined in such a manner that the people crossing the line should see themselves as having moved from a wretched to a slightly better and aspirational state. It is insulting and frustrating for a person to move from a poor to non-poor status without experiencing any difference in his efforts to survive or living conditions.

What is seen in the rural areas of some of the backward states and in most of the cities, especially the metropolitan cities, is appalling. There are millions who live, eat, beg, work, romance, marry, produce children, fall sick, and die without a shelter and without any inkling of where the next meal is going to come from. The plight of this class of people—with access to less than Rs 32 per person per day—is a shade better in rural areas. However, these people have to face discrimination, exploitation, and even criminal intimidation at the hands of the representatives of higher castes and the economically privileged. The large and swelling numbers of people living in poverty and extreme poverty only establishes that there have been no disruptive policies and plans that have been implemented to bring about change in the lives of these people.

A beggar, or even a self-respecting menial worker, who lives under the cover of a plastic sheet on a pavement or a service lane of Mumbai or Delhi has biological urges, like any other human being, and ends up procreating not as a conscious decision but just because he manages to steal an opportunity to sleep with his wife. Children are produced as the result of an opportunity for sexual pleasure and not as a planned activity for starting or increasing the size of the family. However, there is an economic advantage linked to this accidental procreation. The mother starts using the breast-holding baby as a tool for generating some extra guilt-driven sympathy while begging or, if the family is not in the 'business' of begging, the child after five years of age starts contributing something to the family income by working as a child labourer in one of the factories or tea stalls that exist and flourish (illegally) in the many unorganised or even organised sectors of the economy. India has 12.9 million children in the age group of 7 to 17 years employed or doing unpaid work.[13] For children born in such conditions there is very little to look forward to; they inherit penury and pass it on from one generation to another. As a percentage of the total population, there is a decline in the percentage of population living in poverty and extreme poverty but in absolute terms the numbers are huge and swelling.

Official agencies estimate the population of beggars in India in 2015 at 4.1 lacs.[14] Even if the number is not suppressed—of which the possibility is very high—it is a disgrace that decades after independence, having established democratic institutions and constitutional provisions that provide right to food and education, there should be 2.2 lac men and 1.9 lac[15] women walking the Indian streets imploring people to give them money to keep their body and soul together.

The extent of poverty in the country and the inefficiency of the agencies and institutions that are responsible for the evolution of a healthy society is evident from the fact that 37 out of 1,000 children that are born do not reach 5 years of age.[16] According to the report of The United Nations Inter-Agency

Group for Child Mortality Estimation (UN IGME) released in September 2018, there is some improvement in the under-5 child mortality rate. Now we are at the same level as the global average but lower than our poor neighbours—Bangladesh (30/1000) and Nepal (32/1000).[17] As per the report, in the year 2017, a staggering number of 605,000 children died at the neonate stage (before attaining 28 days of age), 197,000 died before their family could celebrate their first birthday and another 187,000 died before they were five years of age and had just about started developing emotional and social connect with their parents and family.

Health economists and public health professionals working for the government and its institutions can easily and convincingly demonstrate that we have done wonderfully well in improving child mortality; we have reduced it from 126/1000 in 1990 to 37/1000 in 2018.[18] However, we need to look at ourselves in comparison to Bangladesh and Nepal which have reduced from 144/1000 and 140/1000 to 30/1000 and 32/1000 respectively during the same period. It is an irony that a country which is the fifth largest economy in the world[19] and which is expected to surpass Japan and emerge as the third largest by 2025,[20] has to be on par with some of the poorest countries in the African Continent in respect of performance on child mortality. The disconnect between the size of the economy and the performance on child mortality is glaring when India's performance is compared with the countries that are on par in respect of the size of the economy.[21]

United States of America	7/1000
Peoples Republic of China	9/1000

Japan	3/1000
Germany	4/1000
India	37/1000

There is enough medical evidence to establish that there is a strong correlation between under-5 child mortality and malnutrition. While sixty-eight per cent of the deaths occur due to malnutrition,[22] the other main contributors are pneumonia, malaria and diarrhea, the three diseases that medical science has taken good control over but are directly linked to poverty. Although, it is a given that there is a comprehensive correlation between poverty and child mortality, the politicians and policymakers of the country need to get a little sensitised about the fact that close to 900,000 children die every year before they are five[23] because of the inability of the State to give their parents the wherewithal to provide them with some basic nutrients and medical attention. It is a disgrace that our country's healthcare budget as a percentage of GDP at 1 per cent (2020)[24] should be one of the lowest in the world. A high rate of child mortality comparable to some of the poorest nations of the world is a reflection of our poor healthcare system.

Findings of the various GOI Committees make a very pathetic reading. These lack the empathy and professional commitment to look at poverty from the perspective of providing even some basic human needs such as shelter, education, healthcare, food and sanitation. Providing food that would keep the body and soul together is just not enough. This approach adopted by professional social scientists is reprehensible. If people are poor and deprived and have to encounter multiple challenges that threaten their very existence every day, we need to acknowledge the scale and severity of the problem; only then would we be able to aim at finding a solution for improving their plight. Non-acceptance of a problem and, in fact, trying to justify or camouflage it through time consuming and self-satisfying empirical research findings, is the biggest road-block for poverty alleviation.

The number of people below the poverty line keeps on increasing despite the fact that the impact of inflation is not being taken into account in fixing the poverty line. Ironically, Dearness Allowance is linked to inflation but the income that is supposed to move a person above the poverty line is free from the impact of inflation. If the poverty line were to be reworked, taking into account the inflation in the last five years, the number of people classified as poor would increase significantly. As per the Tendulkar Committee Report, 354 million people accounting for 29.6 per cent of the population were below poverty line in 2009-10. For the same period, the Rangarajan Committee came up with a figure of 454 million and this accounted for 38.2 per cent of the population.[25] It is high time the alarm bells start ringing and reach the ears of the people who continue to turn a deaf ear to the problem.

While successive governments in power over the last six decades have claimed to have made huge strides in various areas (some of these are there to see as well), they seem to have not been able to come to terms with the fact that they need to redefine poverty. Poverty needs to be graded on availability and access of some basic goods and services that would not only ensure survival but also education-triggered development and the ability to resist being pushed back below the poverty line. A large country which takes pride in the scale of its economy, military power, scientific achievements and the demographic dividend that it can generate because of the size of its young population, cannot be using blinds to avoid the sight of poverty, hunger, malnutrition, illness, lack of education, joblessness, etc. Poverty in India is palpable and policymakers need to be sensitised to the problem when evaluating its magnitude at the aggregate level.

The definition of poverty needs to be reworked. As per the in-use definition, an average urban family of 6 persons (self + spouse + 2 children + parents) ceases to be poor if its total worldly income crosses Rs 8,460 (47X30X6) per month. This so called 'non-poor' family has to pay for its shelter, food, sending children to school, medical care, occasional entertainment to divert attention from their miserable state, and provide for all other social obligations and exigencies at the minimal level from this measly amount. It is supposed to provide for all this by adopting some jugglery in home economics that can be best explained by these highly accomplished State-economists. These economists and the government of the day seem to be working on creating a make-believe in these poor and deprived people that they are no longer poor because some empirical study establishes that Rs 47 per person per day is good enough money to survive in Delhi or Mumbai. Poverty alleviation requires that the affected people see a tangible change in their lives, and not merely by moving people from poor to not so poor category trying to make them believe that they are no longer poor. Placebos seem to have found a place in the economic lexicon as well.

Poverty Line, ideally, should be replaced by a 'Poverty Band'. The people falling in this band are the people that need to be worked upon over a period of time through economic policy deployment and affirmative action to get them into the lower middle class category. This is the class of people that is vulnerable and, if not engaged with, would slip down into a state of abject poverty. The lower end of the band should represent family income that is able to provide for food, hygienic shelter, medical care, clothing, school education for two children and public transport. This is substantially more than what is defined presently as the poverty line threshold. An informal survey carried out by the authors accompanied by extensive fact-finding interviews carried out with the marginalised class of people over a two year period revealed that a family of six can manage to survive and provide for these minimal needs in an urban centre if the household income is Rs 25,000 or more per month. This translates to an individual income of about Rs 140 per day per person. If the family size is smaller, the reduction in income is not proportional to the reduction in number of family members.

The corresponding per day income in rural areas is about Rs 85. At the top end of the band would be aspirational individuals and families that are about to cross over to the lower middle class; this means possessing/renting a '*pucca*' house measuring at least 500 square feet, consuming reasonably nutritious food, possessing a mechanised two wheeler, sending their two children to a 'good' school and having medical insurance cover for the family; possessing a small refrigerator and a television set as household amenities, having access to internet and possessing the ability to build some reserves to meet exigencies. The base income for a family of six for this type of living standard, as revealed by the survey, is about Rs 40,000 per month in an urban area—that translates to about Rs 225 per person per day. The corresponding per person amount for the rural areas is about Rs 135.

Poverty needs to be redefined in the context of changing times taking into account the growing aspirations of all classes of the society. On the one hand we have a class of consumers that are driving the market and making it possible to write the India growth story and, on the other, there are a large number of NGOs and voluntary groups that are trying to ferry leftover food and discarded clothes to a section of the starving and near-naked population. It is dichotomous that the obscenely 'rich class' in India gets to interact—on the streets and at the workplace—with the class of people that is poor, deprived and hopeless and, ironically, it does not evoke any sense of regret or empathy, leave alone guilt.

Despite a lot of propaganda-based sloganeering for poverty removal, we have only added to the number of poor in the last six decades. At the same time the growth of consumerism, in addition to creating a huge market for goods and services, has generated a 'demand-desire' in the aspiring poor. This phenomenon, in addition to making the gap between the rich and the poor vulgarly pronounced, has had its social and psychological fallouts which, if not arrested, can result in class conflicts and unrest that can even take a militant dimension.

There were a number of factors that contributed to the British granting independence to India; the one less discussed was that India had ceased to be an economically attractive colony after the loot and plunder that the Britishers carried out over two centuries of their rule. Indian industry had been completely destroyed, agriculture and mining output had declined because of lack of investments and there was absolutely no financial potential in the market to raise capital. Our banks were virtually bankrupt and so were the people. Whatever little was available in the country was taken away by the British during the Second World War, including the food grain stocks, leaving Indians to starve and die. At the time of independence, out of the total population of 390 million, 70 per cent were poor—this meant that 273 million people were below the poverty line.[26]

After seven decades of independence, we have about 400 million in this category of poor. Successive governments tried different economic management models which combined socialistic, left of centre and neo-liberal thought and approach in varying degrees but the end result has been that the number of people living in poverty remains the same. The only consolation is that we have had no famine since the British left. While this is a huge consolation, it is all the more disturbing because in a famine there is shortage of food. But what we are faced with is a situation wherein the State is not able to create adequate income generating opportunities to enable these 400 million poor to access the food required to keep them above the rather callously defined poverty line. On the one hand we have people struggling to go to sleep without food and on the other we have huge quantities of food grains rotting in the state-owned Food Corporation of India godowns. This is good enough reason for all those involved with public policy to hang their heads in shame. In order to benchmark the poverty line correctly, the authors suggest a new definition as under:

> *All those households that generate an aggregate income which is not sufficient to provide the members of the*

> *household access to hygienic living conditions, minimal food and medical care for maintaining their bodies in a healthy condition that is necessary for being productive, and provide education for children, should be considered below poverty line.*

This definition needs to be monetised and given a value which has to be worked out based on regional, urban/rural, cultural and other socio-economic considerations. The concept behind this definition is to segregate such households that face perpetual poverty and have no hope of crossing the line without support from the State.

The concentration of poverty is pronounced in geographical areas that are prone to exploitation by law makers, administrators and landlords who have been brought up in an environment in which feudalism is eulogised. Lack of education also adds to the problem as no informed and structured challenge is posed to the perpetrators of such exploitation. The poor population is concentrated in geographical locations that have a high concentration of tribal, Dalit, farm labour, and casual labour population.

It has been documented that states such as Madhya Pradesh, Chhattisgarh, Uttar Pradesh, Jharkhand, Bihar, Assam, Manipur and Odisha have a higher rate of rural poverty;[27] and one is tempted to correlate the population of tribals in these states to the poverty prevalent. A number of academicians and researchers have attributed poverty in these areas to floods, droughts and other natural calamities. Natural calamities are unfortunate events that the State has to take care of to ensure that loss of life, property and income is minimised, if not avoided. If there is a belief generated that poverty in these areas exists because of calamities, then it is being endorsed that the State is not responsible for the poverty; it is beyond the control of the State. There is also an obvious disparity in the response to natural calamities between states and cities. Floods in Mumbai—whenever these happen, and they happen for just a day or two—are extensively covered by the media. The quality of State response is discussed and criticised in debates, an SOS declared and schools and colleges closed. On the other hand, a flood situation in Assam which renders tens of thousands homeless and causes deaths to hundreds evokes very little response from people within and outside the State. The hallmark of the State's indulgent response is the prime minister, or more often the chief minister, taking the customary aerial assessment of the situation before announcing a relief package which is, invariably, not even enough to provide succour to even a small population that is displaced and in distress. What sort of assessment can be made from such a survey, which is more like a ritual, is for anyone to guess?

According to the Global Hunger Index published in late 2012 by International Food Research Institute, India ranks at the shameful 97th position in the Global Hunger Index. This is truly shameful and deplorable because, at the aggregate level, the country has more than enough food to feed everyone adequately and yet, we have millions of people starving and suffering from malnutrition.

The policy planners do not get moved by hunger-based human suffering or, perhaps, have no clue of how to reach food to the needy people. Six decades of governance, post Nehru era, by democratically elected governments, has not been able to put together the required infrastructure to ensure that 40 per cent of fruits and vegetables and 20 per cent of food grains are not wasted every year.[28] It is estimated that the equivalent of the wheat produced in Australia gets wasted in India every year. The economic policy managers need to design and deploy plans that would generate the economic ability in people to purchase food that is going waste for sustenance and survival.

The main cause of poverty in India is, without doubt, its large population and the rate of its growth. There has been a significant improvement in arresting the rate of growth of population despite the increasing longevity. India is far better than the countries it is clubbed with on malnutrition and child mortality. Our miserable performance in job creation has just not been able to keep pace with the increase in the population of job seekers. We have the highest rate of unemployment in the past 20 years. Centre for Monitoring Indian Economy (CMIE) has estimated the figure of unemployed seeking jobs in 2018 at 31 million. At one time it was said that India's problem was not unemployment but underemployment. Now we are faced with both. Unemployment levels have been steadily increasing particularly in the past few years; they have peaked in 2018. The agony associated with the shortage of jobs is further aggravated by very low/depressed wages.

In India the workforce is divided in two broad categories based on the nature of employment: (a) organised and (b) unorganised. Workforce in the organised sector is that which is employed and registered with establishments such as the government, government undertakings, educational institutions, corporations, hospitals, etc. This category of workmen are, in a way, highly privileged as they are protected by various rules and regulations under various legislations such as the Industrial Disputes Act, Factories Act, Minimum Wages Act, etc. This category of workmen enjoy assured employment, assured monthly salaries/wages, medical cover, provident fund, gratuity, etc. They are also entitled to periodic revision of salaries to cover for inflation and in some cases get growth through increased responsibilities. This segment of the workforce is considered to be a pampered lot but accounts for only a fraction of the country's workforce.

In India, about 45 per cent of the households earned less than Rs 10,000 per month in 2015.[29] The same percentage of households perhaps would be earning Rs 12,000 in 2019. This is much lower than the figure of Rs 18,000 per month for a new recruit in government service recommended by the 7th Pay Commission. It is unbelievable but true that most of the industrial establishments in the organised sector pay wages to the casually employed which are far lower than what has been recommended by the Pay Commission. The casually employed are part of unorganised sector that are unregistered and are not protected by any act or rules so their employers, expectedly, do not bother about the way their workers manage their lives. Pressure to reduce costs results in very low wages for unskilled casual workmen. This is because the number of workmen looking for jobs far exceeds available jobs. Unskilled workmen have no other options but to work for whatever wages that they can get. Even governments—Central as well as State—end up circumventing the provision by employing contractors for doing routine jobs. While contractors bill at the prescribed or higher rates, they employ casuals on wages which are lower than that recommended by the last Pay Commission. It is an accepted norm and practice with manpower contractors to underpay. The concerned people in the government know of these malpractices but prefer to turn a blind eye.

The permanent workmen in the organised sector tend to form unions and thereby acquire strong bargaining power for themselves. Also, various legislations make it impossible to retrench or layoff, so they have the highest level of job security. Unorganised labour, on the other hand, is totally ungoverned except for being protected under the Minimum Wages Act under which minimum daily wages get revised periodically. Minimum wage prescribed is very low and grossly inadequate for survival. Lack of ability to provide fair employment is reflected in the fact that a casual worker ends up earning about one-third of what his counterpart in the organised sector earns. About 90 per cent of India's workforce is employed in the unorganised sector.[30] And, because of the inability of the Government to regulate through suitable legislation which would help get the required productivity from the 10 per cent organised work force, 90 per cent of the casual workforce is subjected to continuous exploitation. There are numerous reports and case studies on how organised workforces have disrupted production and are responsible for low productivity across the board in Indian industry; yet, there is no action towards correcting the situation. This, in fact, is the biggest deterrent for international companies setting up manufacturing facilities in India. Disparity in wages for identical jobs in the organised and unorganised sectors does not get the required attention. And, why should it? It makes enormous economic sense for the businessman to increase profits by reducing the cost of wages, even if it means human exploitation. Successive governments have been overawed by the capability of the capitalist to create wealth and show little or no sensitivity towards these underpaid 'wealth creators' for the capitalists.

A number of analytical studies conducted by individuals and research organisations have established that excessive regulations, legislated ostensibly for protecting the rights and privileges of labour, are the biggest cause for low employment growth in the country. Our labour related administration and regulations have resulted in very high level of labour market rigidity. This has provided encouragement to a parallel economy that prefers to employ workers from the unorganised sector to avoid the complicated and opaque legislations such as Industrial Disputes Act and Trade Unions Act. Changes in labour laws seem to always aim at expanding the scope of benefits for the workers in the organised sector, requiring submission of additional forms and reports to the various government offices as a proof of compliance. Managing labour as per the procedures laid down under law is frustratingly tedious and deviations can be hazardous.

While labour laws do not prohibit retrenchment or layoffs per se, prior permission is required from the State Government even if the action is warranted for good economic reasons. There are some 'black sheep' within the business community who are driven by the desire to take the unethical route and circumvent the legal provisions to deny the workers their rights and work out exit routes without adequately compensating the affected workers. However, the rule-book following honest businessmen who want to close down their operations, because the product or service that they offer has lost its significance with the ultimate consumer, have to struggle for years to get the bureaucratic clearance for doing so. It is not only the process they have to go through but the uncertainty about the decision that would be announced at the end of the frustratingly long and laborious procedure that makes the process unviable.

Indian labour laws are restrictive. This is the opinion expressed by experts over the years and their voice is getting louder every day. In fact, these laws are categorised as the most restrictive in comparison to those prevailing in the other developed and developing economies. India's private sector, including its organised manufacturing sector, employs about 10 million people.[31] Indian firms need to obtain government permission to lay off if they employ more than 100 workers.[32] This partly explains why most Indian firms are and remain small. In India, 70 per cent of employment in the organised manufacturing sector in 2016 was in firms with less than 6 employees. As against this, about 45 per cent of the urban workforce in China in 2011 was employed in individual business and small enterprises.[33] Small manufacturing firms cannot take advantage of the economy of scale or use latest technology and, hence, suffer from low productivity. These slowly, but surely, move towards closure since the operating environment provides competition from the few who have shown the courage to increase capacity and productivity to global standards. In addition, there are manufacturers in countries like China who are recognised as market disruptors across the globe.

Our laws are the biggest roadblock for workmen seeking organised sector employment. Indian business establishments have consistently opted for expensive equipment and automation for productivity improvement when the same could be achieved through additional labour inputs. In the last 10 years increase in employment per unit increase in GDP has dropped. There has been a distasteful and noisy debate that one has witnessed about the methodology of calculation of GDP and employment in the recent past. Assuming that the debate is uncalled for and the numbers shared by the government are honestly estimated and correct, there is reason to be concerned. If the GDP in 2018-19 has grown at 7 per cent and is expected to grow at 7.6 per cent in 2019-20 and, at the same time, there is a mass-scale anxiety about unemployment and underemployment, there is reason to believe that we need to revisit our economic policies to factor in employment generation as one of the main objectives for growth. Jobless growth or a low job growth to GDP growth ratio is a clear indication of policies and programmes of the government being skewed in favour of the capitalist—something for which the opposition is blaming the present day government. Interestingly, the opposition seems to find it convenient to forget that in UPA I (2004-2009) while the GDP grew at a CAGR of 8.7 per cent per annum, jobs grew at an abysmal 0.1 per cent per annum.[34] In India we have a large population of unemployed people and an equally large population of employed, but frustrated people chasing only GDP growth without commensurate growth in employment. This is deplorable and shameful as it not only suppresses achievable GDP growth but also generates unease and unrest.

The most important underlying factors for low growth in manufacturing sector and an insignificant growth in employment generation in this sector is the 'legal inhibitor' that has been unwittingly put in place. The government needs to enact a new set of laws that would convert the casually employed into organised workforce to make them reasonably secure. It would give freedom to firms that want to layoff on becoming unviable or even for other valid reasons. If all labour belongs to the organised sector and it is ensured that their wages and benefits are as per the prescribed norms, the fear of the fallout of layoffs would cease to be an issue. For the sake of protecting the small group of people who are presently employed, growth in employment cannot be sacrificed. There is enough hunger in the Indian entrepreneurs and businessmen to set up facilities and grow to global scales of operation if restrictive legal framework were not there causing big hurdles that businessmen find difficult to negotiate.

Make in India is, conceptually, a very sound idea but unfortunately, has not yet yielded any tangible results. Manufacturing creates a lot of employment for various types of people—unskilled, skilled, and managerial. China made itself the world's manufacturing base and is a great example for us to follow. The trade war between USA and China and increasing labour costs in China provide us a great window to get international companies to shift their shops to India. We should not lose this opportunity.

Even after sixty years, we are unable to bring down the number of people below the poverty line in absolute numbers and have to get into a self-congratulatory mode by taking refuge in the argument that poverty in percentage terms has come down. Today, even that is not true. With our large and growing population, it is fallacious to believe that the existing policy regime that works on the basis of a trickle-down effect for the elimination of poverty is going to get the desired results. A conventional approach can only deliver conservative results.

Our problem is much too large to depend upon current policies to deliver worthwhile tangible results.

Poverty elimination needs a radical and focused approach that would break the vicious cycle; this can be done only if we are able to find a way to create jobs for all job seekers in the country. If this were to happen, we may suffer a drop in productivity per person but would still increase our GDP dramatically. As a rule, savings get generated in every economic cycle created by every individual; as the money goes around, the demand for consumption increases. Capital created through savings of every individual gets deployed to meet the extra demand. This, in turn, creates additional jobs. In the recent past, not only has our rate of savings dropped but the jobs created per unit increase in GDP have also come down. Both these phenomena have played havoc with new job creation. What we fail to take into account is that all the unemployed 31 million[35] (an underestimated number) and their dependents continue to survive because of social support provided by family and friends. If these good souls did not have to support those unemployed, they would be saving the money for themselves. It is, therefore, justified to employ the unemployed even on jobs where the productivity is compromised.

The most progressive and radical step taken by the previous government has been the legislating and implementing the Mahatma Gandhi National Rural Employment Guarantee Act (MGNREGA). This guarantees 100 days of work to a rural household whose members volunteer to do unskilled labour work. In the last thirteen years, MGNREGA and its earlier version National Rural Employment Guarantee Act (NREGA), have reached out to millions of households in the rural areas. The success of the programme is evident from the fact that in the year 2018-19, it is estimated that 2,550 million days of employment were provided.[35] The inference from this number is that there is huge distress in rural areas. As per the Comptroller and Auditor General (CAG) report, only an average of 52.02 man-days of employment per person was provided between 2012-13 and 2016-17.[36] It was revealed that the low performance was because the annual development plan and labour budget were not approved in time and quorum for approval by the Gram Sabha was not fulfilled. If we were to assume that the employment under the scheme in 2018-19 also remained as it was in the five year period between 2012-13 and 2016-17 i.e., 52.2 man-days per person, then the number of people employed under the scheme is a staggering 49 million. There can be no better indicator of rural distress than the fact that 49 million households, at the rate of five persons per household (245 million people), benefitted from the scheme. This represents 30 per cent of the rural population who have to send one of their members for casual unskilled employment. The situation is alarming and warrants serious thought and meaningful intervention.

What is required is a strong political will supported by some innovative fiscal management that would enable the State governments to provide employment under MGNREGA or a similar programme not limited to 100 days per household. The employment should be for everyone between 18 and 58 years of age, for as many days as he/she desires to work, at a wage rate determined by an independent body which has been given a clear mandate to ensure that through these wages there would have to be a distinct up-gradation in the standards of nourishment, healthcare and education of the children of the participants of the scheme. Those employed should have the means to move above the defined poverty line.

Every human being is an asset as long as he has a job and earns his own livelihood. Otherwise, he is a liability to be fed, sheltered and clothed by others. An employed person pays for himself instead of someone else paying his living expenses. When he works, he not only pays for his own liabilities but also creates some surplus (savings). When he works without using any capital his output is poor but when supported by capital, his output increases. The increase in output is proportionate to the quantum of capital employed. It thus stands to reason that it is beneficial for the country to have every human being employed fruitfully, even if it is without capital as opposed to have him sitting idle and someone else paying for his living expenses. Whatever he earns when employed shows up as the GDP by a multiple of more than one.

Let us take an example to highlight the advantage of using human capital for asset creation. Suppose a village requires a water body of say 100,000 cubic meters and there exists a required catchment area to fill this water body when it rains. This water body, once created, becomes a valuable asset available for use of the whole village. The asset can easily be given an economic value based on price of water and quantum of storage. Assume that 300 people organised under an umbrella of a cooperative (legally formed under appropriate statutes) got together to complete the job and this cooperative of 300 members took about a year to create the required water body. A suitable method could be worked out such that these people got paid only 60 per cent of the wages in cash and balance 40 per cent is apportioned towards the ownership of water in the water body. Workers become shareholders in the cooperative in proportion to the number of days each worker has worked and the cooperative becomes the owner of the water body. The forty per cent, so contributed towards building the pond, becomes net capital formation for the cooperative as also for the community. This particular cooperative of 300 members can move from place to place to create similar water bodies at other places as per the requirement of the villages to be vetted by an expert body of the government. Over a period of time these cooperatives will start owning some basic tools for doing the same job with improved efficiency. The process should be such that the wages paid in cash are sufficient for the worker to meet his minimal needs. There should be no compromise on the total wage paid to them. Total wage should be equal to or more than that suggested by the Pay Commission from time to time, or such that the household remains above the defined poverty line. The capital asset so formed by the cooperative becomes a large part of savings of the members to meet the requirements of their children and also for their old age. More importantly, this should break the vicious cycle of poverty for people in this group who are members of the given cooperative. There should be thousands of such cooperatives in our country. Digging ponds and building roads is not the only job these cooperatives can do. The concept can be extended to other useful national assets formation. Another very important expected outcome is that the 300 workmen who have worked to create these assets are now part of an organised work force having security of job and also some savings.

MGNREGA is essentially a programme to provide some

livelihood to those who have no jobs so no means of survival. The Act provides employment for a limited number of days at a prescribed daily wage to only those who qualify a certain criteria. Wages are required to be paid within a specified period. The law makes it necessary that delayed payment should attract interest after a lapse of a specified period. The programme is not really working, as was intended, for various reasons. The incumbent government's view initially was that this was a necessary evil and a waste of money. The Union Budget does not provide sufficient funds to meet the universal requirement to employ all those who demand and require this help. According to reports, the Central Government does not transfer money on timely basis to States for successfully running the programme. The states, also, take their own time to release payments to the beneficiaries. Reports claim that wages are delayed and this period is at an average of 50 days,[37] and yet, the interest on delays is not paid. The Union Budget for 2020-21 allocated Rs 61,500 crores for this programme.[38] The programme is primarily for people who are living in conditions of severe poverty. Despite the fact that the Act has been in force for over seven years, the implementation is more in letter and not in spirit. It is unfortunate that our politicians as well as bureaucrats, as a rule, show very little concern for victims of extreme poverty.

The programme is meant to provide livelihood to the needy poor and should not be considered as charity. Effective utilisation of these people is the business of those running the programme. Their yield is dependent upon the type of job provided to them under different schemes. It is the government's job to make them work on schemes that create assets which have a definite economic value. Considering that this group consists of people who are unskilled or at best semi-skilled, the assets to be created should be such that communities are prepared to pay for the use of these assets. The South-West Monsoon in our country lasts for about four months, from mid-June to September. More than 75 per cent of our rainfall occurs in this period.[39] The fate of kharif crop depends on monsoon. Good rains during this period result in bountiful harvest. About fifty per cent of crops in India are completely dependent on monsoon and the rest on the man-made irrigation system. This makes our country highly vulnerable to vagaries of nature. These vagaries have increased in the recent past due to climate changes. Though our country receives a lot of water through snow-fed rivers, it is estimated that over 40 per cent of rain water gets drained into sea.[40] If we were able to reduce drainage into sea by 10 per cent, we would be able to mitigate problems that we face due to insufficient rains. Creating water storage facilities is something that can be easily achieved by utilising people employed under MGNREGA.

Every state should have a list of quantified storage facilities with identified catchment area for the purpose. Every storage facility should have a declared asset value depending upon the quantity of water the facility can store. The aim should be to see that in case of failure of rains, stored water is sufficient to meet the needs of farming, drinking and other household and industrial requirements within the designated area. The facility and water could be owned by the cooperative of workmen who create the storage facility. Those who have created the facility would be paid only 60 per cent in cash and the balance through sale of water for say 15 years of the completion of the storage.

Use of water should be charged and the community should pay for the quantity of water drawn. This ensures permanent availability of water in the future. Charges for water should, obviously, be reasonable. After 15 years, the ownership of the facility and the water should be transferred to the community. To achieve this overall objective, we need to have suitable cooperatives, and learning from the success of India's milk and sugar cooperatives can help define the operating framework. Each state could have a number of such cooperatives depending upon the number and size of such facilities to be created.

Unskilled and semi-skilled employed under MGNREGA could also be employed to create housing for the poor, construction of proper drainage system in the villages, internal village roads, etc. Village governing bodies could have their own plans for such projects. All projects must be such that their use creates revenue for paying 40 per cent of the unpaid salary to those who have created these assets. Village governing bodies need to have access to capital from banks to buy material for creating these assets. Material cost could be recovered from those who use these facilities. Additional funds required for removing the cap of 100 days of employment could be funded by abolishing the Corporate Social Responsibility (CSR) tax of 2 per cent of the profits by diverting the same to this scheme.

We could also look for other such opportunities available around us. India's largest and Asia's second largest earthen dam—Bansura Sagar Dam—in the state of Kerala was built in 1979 by workmen employed in thousands with very little capital equipment support.

We have a gigantic project which has been under discussion for over 50 years but because of its mind boggling scale in terms of volume of work and cost, it continues to remain on the drawing board. The project of creating a "National Water Grid" was first proposed by Dr KL Rao, a dam designer in 1970s. The Prospective Plan under the scheme envisions water storage facilities like dams and barrages for around 185 billion cubic meters of water.[41] The plan envisages linking of these water storage bodies and transporting the water to wherever needed in the country by creating more than 30 canals covering thousands of kilometers all across the country. The project, besides providing irrigation to additional 35 million hectares of land, will generate 40,000 MW of clean/green energy. It envisions flood control in the flood prone areas by diverting excess water to areas which are prone to droughts.

There is yet another advantage—water grids can provide thousands of kilometers of navigational waterways for transporting goods; this means of transport is expected to be one-half in cost as against transportation by road/rail.[42] Overall transportation value in our country is about 14 to 15 per cent of GDP (perhaps the highest in the world); in China it is just about 11.6 per cent. Building waterways will create a very significant cost advantage for our economy, not to mention the distinct advantage emanating from the improvement in the air quality. The project has been split into three parts geographically: a) Himalayan rivers inter-ink; b) Peninsular component; and c) Inter-state links. The project is being managed by National Water Development Agency (NWDA). This agency has prepared reports on 14 inter-links for Himalayan region, 16 inter-links for Peninsular and 37 inter-links for inter-states.

The project, no doubt mammoth in size, has huge cost implications and is a big challenge for implementation. But, considering that it has the potential to change the face of our country in respect of irrigation for secured farming, power generation, transportation, flood control, providing water to drought prone areas, the project should have moved high on the priority list. Why nothing has happened is a serious concern. No government has shown the courage, conviction and the foresight to start allocating money for this in their annual budgets to commence work. The purpose of discussing this project is to bring into focus the fact that while enumerating the advantages of the project, the important aspect of the additional jobs that this project will create has not been highlighted. We have a burning problem of unemployment in our country that can be solved if we were to decide to implement the scheme. The problem of unemployment has stunted our growth in the recent past and will continue to haunt us even in the foreseeable future, unless we find a pragmatic and sustainable solution. This project is a very large civil engineering project involving billions of cubic meters of earthwork that can be easily made very labour intensive. By making it labour intensive, tens of millions of semi-skilled and unskilled jobs can be created, along with tens of thousands of jobs for the educated in engineering, accounting, administration, etc. Not only will we create jobs but will also provide an enormous boost to our GDP growth rate through increased consumption. The project will take decades to implement and lacs of crores of rupees of budget allocation. We will be able to provide jobs under MGNREGA to as many people who are willing to work for as many days they are willing to contribute for decades to come. We can even look at the possibility of making labour partners in this scheme if we are looking to limit the cash outgo. For our country, this would be a real leap forward. We also believe that we have sufficiently smart people who would be able to find ways to generate extra funds internally or through borrowings needed for this visionary scheme.

Post 1991, the Indian policymakers and the managers of the national economy have mastered the art of generating a decent GDP growth number. This was a healthy change from the Hindu rate of growth (a term so appropriately coined by late Prof Raj Krishna, a Professor at Delhi School of Economics) that linked the fatalistic and contended cultural approach of Hindus to performance. The fillip to the economy was provided by the reforms unleashed by the then Finance Minister, Manmohan Singh, who was fully supported by the then Prime Minister, Narasimha Rao. Both of them had little or no political following but have left a lasting impression on the minds of people. Steps taken by these two proved to be gamechangers for the Indian economy. Unfortunately, Narasimha Rao, the founder of modern India is completely forgotten as a result of the orchestrated scheme of the power centre in the Congress Party to not remember him as a great leader; and Manmohan Singh has been ridiculed into oblivion for his soft and quiet approach by his political opponents.

The Indian economy has been on the upswing and has emerged as one of the fastest growing economies of the world. While this is celebrated in political circles as something that people should be proud of, there is a rather feeble attempt to see the incongruity between growth and deprivation. About half the population of the country is unaffected by the growth numbers. GDP and its growth numbers have absolutely no meaning for them as their fate is permanently sealed and they have no means of breaking their 'fate-wall'. There are a minuscule number who do jump over this wall. They become the poster boys for the publicity campaigns of the proclaimed vibrant economic management policies that we have had under successive governments and which we, erroneously, think provide the so-called equal opportunities to everyone. The poor and deprived will experience a perpetual status quo unless they are integrated into the economic mainstream; this can happen only if we are able to design and deploy policies that engage and empower them.

The fundamental question that we need to ask ourselves and the people we elect to govern us is 'who does the country belong to?' Wealth is created when capital and labour are applied to natural resources, which are provided free to us by nature, for making marketable products. Only people with capital have the ability and the wherewithal to indulge in this so called wealth creation phenomenon. This growing trend of the wealthy becoming wealthier is staring us in the face and, before long, the victims of this growth will give a blow to the exploiters of the system. The distribution of wealth has become skewed because of economic mismanagement that finds its roots in continually degenerating moral and ethical standards of the society as a whole.

The fundamental elements of a country are its territory, people, natural resources, and the government. All the natural resources of the country are owned collectively by the citizens of the country and the government is the custodian of these resources. Every citizen has equal ownership right over these natural resources. These are available to us in many shapes and forms like coal, crude oil, iron ore, bauxite, limestone, marble, granite, air waves, atmospheric air, etc. The list of useful natural resources is very long but these are not given any book value even though they have very high intrinsic value. They are passed on to its users through the process of auction. So, there is an inherent dichotomy in the entire process as resources that belong to every citizen of the nation get acquired by an individual or a group of individuals with deep pockets. Since the number of such wealthy people is very small and they are driven by the common interest of wealth maximisation, cartelisation is an effective tool for them to manage the bidding process in a manner in which the asset can be acquired at a substantially low value.

The next step for these people is to convert these resources into marketable products; for doing this they use cheap unorganized labour sourced through contractual manipulations, using the options made available by the government through various skill development and other schemes at about one-third, or even less, of the wages of the organised labour. Low cost of procurement of a natural resource coupled with an exploitation level labour cost leaves huge margins for these businessmen or companies. This is precisely the reason why the mineral rich States of Odisha, Jharkhand and Chhattisgarh have remained poor while those states that are into value-addition activities have become rich. The whole phenomenon does not only reflect the loopholes in the policy and its administration but also the complete lack of respect the exploiters of the system show for ethics and morality. The country and her people are getting short-changed and looted in the process as a result of the nexus between the capitalists, politicians and the bureaucracy. The nexus blatantly allows the acquisition of natural resources at ridiculously low prices and violates the provisions of minimum wages prescribed in the 7th Pay Commission.

A problem that existed a century back has, instead of being resolved, taken a stronger foothold. Jawaharlal Nehru in his 1929 AICC Presidential Address in Lahore had said: "Our economic programme must, therefore, be based on a human outlook and must not sacrifice man to money. If an industry cannot be run without starving its workers, then the industry must close down. If the workers on the land have not enough to eat, then the intermediaries who deprive them of their full share must go. The least that every worker in field or factory is entitled to is a minimum wage which will enable him to live in moderate comfort and humane hours of labour which do not break his strength and spirit...."[43]

The fact is that very poor people do not get to use any manufactured products as these are beyond their means. Ironically, products manufactured from cheaply acquired natural resources, when converted into manufactured goods by using cheap and exploited labour, are just not affordable for the very people who produce these goods. There is a definite case to show that the government has no lien on what it collects from the sale of natural resources. The money belongs to every citizen of the county. The government needs to sell natural resources at a fair price which should be arrived at by using a model that takes into consideration the class of downstream products that are manufactured from these resources, and the price sensitivity of the products produced—and not a throwaway price for political considerations or expediency. The amount thus collected should be distributed equally to all the poor citizens of the country. The simple logic for this is that if a resource that belongs equally to a set of people is sold, the proceeds must be distributed equally amongst the owners.

Though the resources come free, these have a significant underlying economic value which is beyond the market value determined by supply and demand equation of our country alone. If we were to import a mineral whose landed price is higher than the prevailing local price, then the imported price and not the local price would be the underlying value of the mineral. The underlying value gets realised by only those who actually use the products made from these free resources. Those who use cars, motorcycles, home appliances, and other products that use steel, for example, tend to get a subsidy because the true underlying value of the resource has not been built into the final cost of the product. But those who are poor and do not have access to such products, lose out on the benefit accruing out of the lower purchase value of free natural resources of the country. It is reasonable to assign the actual economic underlying value of each natural resource and levy the same as a cess at the point of mining of the resource. Steel, for example, is used in one form or the other by everyone from lower middle class to the rich. If we were to levy a nominal cess of say Rs 500 per tonne on approximately 400 million tonnes of iron ore that we currently mine per annum, we would collect Rs 20,000 crores of this cess annually, in addition to the GST on the sale of the final steel product. If because of this process, the cost of steel and steel products goes up, so be it, because the impact on the cost of the final product would be negligible. Similarly, there are a lot of other resources that can be taxed (including air and water). We could end up with a substantial pool of this cess which would be available for direct transfer to the needy. In doing so, our policymakers must not see this as a dole or a subsidy to the people for their sustenance but as an access to the money that belongs to them and over which they have all the right.

The philosophy of Universal Basic Income which is gaining widespread acceptance has little meaning in the Indian context as our society is divided into classes which are quite disparate. It makes absolutely no sense for the State to distribute money to people who belong to the privileged class. The principle that should be used is that the underlying value of the resource should be distributed amongst people who do not get to use such resource even indirectly. The money in the hands of needy would increase national consumption level substantially and, in turn, improve the GDP considerably.

Our economic management and developmental model needs to go through a comprehensive realignment. From a socialistic model which was adopted till the early 1990s we have gone to a cold capitalistic model without taking into account the diverse needs of the nation. Western capitalism has evolved over a long period of time and, thereby, has adjusted to the needs of the people of individual countries. We adopted the Western capitalistic model without being ready for it. The shift to something that was not developed on home ground and which was not taken through an evolutionary-process was bound to leave some unattended problems. It was like a group of starved people being made to sit in a fine-dining European restaurant and offered a multi-course dinner. It was too complex a situation for them to handle. It offered opportunities for some people who were familiar with the use of the 'policy cutlery' kept on the table, but most of the people remained hungry because of not being prepared to eat in such an environment.

Insofar as our deployment of capital is concerned, it seems to be targeted at satisfying the demand of consumers. No complaints about that but the application of classical capitalist dictum to our labour market has caused havoc. It has left a large part of our labour force as beggars having to accept whatever is offered to them in the form of wages because of the inaction of the authorities.

These people end up just about surviving at the animal level. They perpetuate poverty leaving very little hope for them to get out of the vicious cycle of poverty. If this is the fate of a large percentage of our population, with no change in sight, what consolation can be derived from the fact that we have a high GDP growth rate or that we are the fastest growing economy in the world. What Nehru said ninety years back should haunt us as we are nowhere close to giving wages that would allow the workers to provide for the "minimum requirements to lead a respectable healthy life". He had said that if this is not possible it is "better that the industry is shut down". An operational institution has been created that is diametrically opposite of what Nehru had visualised and proposed. Labour exploitation has reached immoral standards and all those establishments that are indulging in this are growing in number and size, leave alone shutting down. In fact, labour exploitation seems to have become a necessary tool for growth. It might not be out of place to assume that we might reach a level at which even the nationalised banks would not consider processing business proposals for financing if the financial projections are worked out on the basis of labour being paid the statutory minimum wages. Labour exploitation seems to have become the unstated mandatory condition for even business houses that are considered as role models for start-ups and have wormed their way up into becoming a voice in industry associations and government committees.

Classical capitalistic system requires that a small percentage of available workforce is kept without jobs to ensure that the supply of labour is always marginally more than demand. The level at which this number should be varies from one economist to another but they all want it to be in the range of 4 to 5 per cent of the available workforce. This includes 2 per cent that do not want to work at all for their individual reasons. This level of unemployment is very actively guarded and kept within the range. In most progressive countries, the unemployed have safety nets; these vary from country to country and are linked to the poverty line standards of the country. In USA the poverty threshold is defined as USD 12,760 per person (65 years of age) per year.[44] In India, households with this income level belong to middle class on the basis of purchasing power parity. Our present population of unemployed is more than 35 million which is about 9 per cent of the employed.[45] It is a paradox that growth in jobs per unit growth of GDP has been decreasing continuously. With increasing population of the country this number of unemployed will keep on growing with time. As the number of unemployed increases, the supply of labour, which is already high compared to demand, will become even more skewed with time and will drive wages even lower. The impact on wages in the exploitative labour market could become a cause of concern for the human rights activists. We seem to be moving towards the use of captive labour (almost bonded) just as our British colonialists did in India not very long ago.

We have to shake ourselves up from our slumber for a radical transformation.

It is important to recognise that in the Indian context it is inconceivable to have market forces determine wages and expect that labour exploitation would not be rampant. It would, in fact, drive wages to a level that would create conditions of starvation of the working people. The first step should be fixing of minimum wages for our millions of casual labour who happen to comprise 90 per cent of our workforce, and putting together a strong administrative mechanism to ensure that it is implemented effectively. This wage, obviously, needs to be indexed with inflation and the underlying philosophy for fixing the minimum wages should be what Nehru had said. In today's context, it would perhaps be in the range of Rs 25,000 to Rs 30,000 per month depending upon the city with all the benefits like provident fund and adequate medical insurance cover for the whole family. The wage should be such that the family can afford to educate children and enable them to progressively move above the poverty line defined earlier. In addition to ensuring that the workforce gets standard and regulated wages, it is important to see that they become an organised and structured workforce. Organised structure does not necessarily mean unionised. The kind of protection that the current legal framework provides to the labour force has proved to be disastrous. We need to have an operating system that ensures that the worker gets what is due to him; the premise here is that what is due needs to be redefined first. At the same time, the expectation in operating efficiency has to be clearly agreed and adhered to. Exploitation can be restricted, and eventually eradicated only if laws are formulated that ensure fair wages.

Capitalism in the western world has produced some great philanthropists; this has happened because these people realised the importance of giving back something to the society by making sure that the underprivileged also became a part of the economic mainstream. In India, philanthropy finds its roots in guilt dilution. There is enough evidence in public domain about the involvement of Indian businessmen in white collar crimes, even criminal activity. The conspicuous display of the charity given by them for building and managing temples and other socio-religious activities is an indication.

We have two problems at hand: a) strengthening and regulating the unorganised sector: and b) creating more jobs. The best option, perhaps, is to promote labour cooperatives to suit individual requirements. We have a very large unorganised labour force employed in farming, transport, manufacturing, construction, housekeeping, domestic services, etc. In the recent past, e-retailers have emerged as a large employer for such people. Considering the large spectrum of jobs/functions that the labour force has to perform, there will have to be different forms and types of cooperatives. Farm labour would perhaps be at the taluka/district level with manufacturing—company wise, transport/ports—trade wise, etc. Fortunately in India, in her history of a little more than a hundred years, the cooperative sector has evolved and matured considerably and is capable of working out models set up to cater to the various sectors of the economy in different geographical and socio-economic conditions. The objective of these cooperatives should be: a) not to allow the employers to exploit the employees and to function with minimum bureaucratic or any other interference; b) must promote healthy team work between employees; c) reward employees for generating improved results; and d) provide wages that meet the standards defined earlier. At the same time, there should be no guarantee of service. The employer should have the liberty of dismissing an employee found inefficient or non-productive. Since the objective is to protect the workforce from the influence of supply and demand for determining wages, one standard basic wage which is indexed to the inflation rate of essential household commodities should be arrived at.

Every human being is a liability if unemployed. Once employed, he becomes economically independent and does not require support for sustenance if he is paid properly. He also starts saving in some form or the other. Having become an independent earner, his consumption levels increase and as a consumer he creates yet another individual economic cycle. A million additionally employed hands create a million additional consumption cycles. If we were to employ every able-bodied person willing to work, we would be creating millions of individual economic cycles of demand. Able-bodied persons will help increase our country's GDP in proportion to the number of additional people employed. Growth, so created, will be inclusive in the real sense of the word. There are a number of growth models used by different developing countries depending upon their individual needs. People's Republic of China, for example, chose the model which is based on employment generation. Our country, which also has a large population, requires a similar growth model. Unless we find our own ways of employing the continually increasing number of unemployed, we would be consigning more and more people to live in poverty.

According to the Centre for Monitoring Indian Economy (CMIE), the number of employed has not shown improvement in the last few years. The quarter of January–March 2017 suffered 1.5 million losses of jobs in comparison to the preceding quarter (October–December 2016), apparently due to demonetization on 8 November 2016. The implementation of the not so well thought through GST pushed back the recovery of jobs even further. It is quite clear that our count of unemployed is increasing at an alarming rate because of: a) lack of creation of new jobs; and b) increasing number of people wanting jobs due to population growth. The reasons for lack of new jobs are: a) slowdown in new investments; b) increased automation; c) closing down of unprofitable companies; and d) large scale consolidation in various industries because of accumulation of non-performing assets by the banks; these banks also being under pressure to consolidate for survival. All these factors are taking a huge toll on our labour market which is already in a precarious condition. The problem faced by labour is of sub-sustenance level wages. The lack of opportunities for employment coupled with a distorted wage structure has enormous political repercussions.

While CMIE puts the number of people currently unemployed at 35 million, according to Organization for Economic Cooperation and Development (OECD), over 30 per cent of our youth is unemployed and only 23.5 per cent of the female population in India is in employment. These figures put together by these credible agencies have reached the public domain and yet no one has given a figure of the total number who could be employed but remain unemployed. Ironically, our overall labour participation rate is less than 50 per cent.[46] Labour force participation represents total employed plus unemployed that are looking to work divided by total population above the age of 15 years. Our 50 per cent participation rate is very poor compared to China where this figure is close to 68 per cent.[47] From this figure one can draw only one conclusion—we have millions who have given up even seeking jobs because: a) they do not see any job opportunities; b) jobs generate very low income; and c) when men of the household are unemployed, their women do not even try for employment. It appears that about 20 per cent of the employable work force is not even seeking jobs.

The obvious conclusion that one draws is that if we were to create sufficient employment opportunities at a proper rate of wages/salaries, we could have another 150 million women/men seeking jobs. What is very worrisome is that we have a growth which is only monetary capital driven and has nothing to do with our vast human capital. We have completely ignored the fact that we can increase our GDP by a significant number through use of human capital while continuing with the use of monetary capital. Human beings are also a capital and it is in the interest of the nation to employ as many people as possible.

China invited hundreds of international companies to set up manufacturing facilities by offering them cheap labour, leased land and logistic and administrative facilitation. This was in early 1980s. Companies were asked to bring their own capital and markets for selling products produced in China. This is how China started its journey toward becoming a superpower purely by utilising her human capital with concerted determination. India and China were almost similarly placed as recently as 1990 with a per capita GDP of USD 367 and 318 respectively.[48] After its struggle in the initial few decades, China hit upon a winning idea which it pursued single-mindedly. Today, China's per capita GDP is close to five times that of India—China is at USD 10,262 while India is at USD 2,104.[49] China produces and consumes over ten times more steel, an important measure of development, than us. They have created an infrastructure which is far advanced than any other country in the world and have, by and large, succeeded in removing poverty. Their approach was to eradicate poverty by using their human resources along with some small infusion of their own capital while we considered our population as a drag on the economy and never thought of using it for increasing wealth.

The biggest impediment towards creating jobs in the manufacturing sector has been our legislative framework. Indian firms are just not able to scale up their capacity to global standards and improve their competitiveness and viability and profitability. While labour leaders seem to be uncompromising on the question of labour reforms, our successive governments, and even the politicians in the opposition, have lacked the courage and conviction to make (or even suggest) amendments that would provide the growth impetus to the manufacturing sector which would prove beneficial for the labour force as well. This problem has been on the table of various governments for more than four decades and there is still no solution that seems to be emerging. There seems to be a vested political interest in maintaining the status quo; this would probably change only when economic advantages of change are perceived to generate political advantage or are able to offset its political fallout.

It is unbelievable that there is an ongoing lack of action by governments to reform laws and make these logical and reasonable for the employers as well. If, for whatever reason, the government finds it difficult to change laws, it is time to accept this as a political reality that has to be lived with. The government could define a cut-off date and all those employed prior to the defined date could be governed by the set of existing laws and rules. For people employed after the cut-off date, there could be new laws that are benchmarked to international standards. This would make India an attractive destination for investments in the manufacturing sector. A number of international companies have explored options of setting up manufacturing facilities in India but developed cold feet primarily because of our stifling labour laws.

We can easily make India a manufacturing hub. It is still not too late. If new laws are enacted which are reasonable and practical, and acceptable to the new employees as well as employers, "Make in India" would not be a pipe dream. Millions of jobs would be created through this process. It would also relieve the government of the burden of training people for industry as it would train its own people to suit its own requirements.

International companies wanting to start manufacturing in India face problems in not being able to get the required land for setting up the facilities. This, of course, is a smaller problem. Some states have been able to mitigate this and are able to provide satisfactory solutions to prospective manufacturers. Other states need to simply emulate the operating model of these states. Getting international companies that find it difficult to continue their manufacturing operations in China—and there are many—to shift their operations to India should be pursued vigorously and wholeheartedly. Bangladesh and a few other neighbourhood countries are already doing this. No company would want to close down operations unless they find it impossible to continue. A lot of money is lost in closing down operations. It must be assumed that their need to close down is very real.

In addition to direct employment, manufacturing generates significant indirect employment. For everyone employed in the manufacturing sector, on an average another four jobs are created outside the manufacturing premises.[51] Wages in China have been rising quite steeply in the past ten years. It is reported that the average wage in China for an industrial worker is about Rs 64,500[52] per month and the corresponding figure for India is a meagre Rs 16,000.[53] Even if we were to pay Rs 30,000 per month there still is a huge incentive for international manufacturing companies to consider India for setting up their operations. This can happen if we either modify our existing labour laws or enact a new labour law regime for all those employed after a cut-off date. Another serious obstacle that the international companies face is bureaucratic red tapism. To begin with, we must recognise and admit that Indian bureaucracy is notoriously famous for having created and nurtured frustrating standards in red tapism. It can get exasperating for investors to spend months, which could extend to years, for getting the land and other required clearances and permissions. These must be provided in the shortest possible time and, preferably, through a single window operation, just as it is done in China.

Loss of time is loss of money, opportunity, and increased cost of project and this is obviously not acceptable to investors. The Central and State governments need to act proactively. If India has to emerge as a manufacturing hub and grow as fast as China did in the earlier years, just growing at the current rate will not serve the purpose. China's labour force participation rate of 68 per cent has helped Chinese households with higher income and higher household consumption.[54] To reach the Chinese level of labour participation rate, we need to create 150 million additional jobs over and above the 450 million jobs that are in place. Since for every job created in the organised manufacturing sector four jobs get created outside, we have to create only about 35 million formal jobs in the manufacturing sector to generate employment for 150 million people.

In the last four years, we seem to have lost our focus from exports. In 2003, the Government of the day started working on pushing exports in real earnestness to increase the nation's GDP. The next government continued with its efforts in the same direction even more vigorously. In 2003-2004 our merchandise exports valued USD 45 billion[55] (Chinese exports in the same year 2003 were USD 383 billion,[56] more than 8 times our exports). Exports represented 10.55 per cent of India's GDP. From then on, our exports grew by 21 per cent every year for 10 years reaching USD 312.4 billion in 2013-14.[57] This remarkable achievement increased the share of exports to 17 per cent of GDP. For two years thereafter, we faltered and went down to USD 275 billion in 2016-17.[58] There was a marginal improvement to USD 303 billion in 2017-18[59] representing 11.6 per cent of GDP. If we had continued to grow our exports at 15-16 per cent, our exports would have been almost USD 580 billion in 2018-19. The difference between the figures of what should have been achieved and what was actually achieved is USD 277 billion for the year 2018-19. This loss has meant a hit of almost 1 per cent of the GDP for the year. Even more damaging was the loss of opportunity for additional 4 million jobs. With unemployment, poverty and hunger staring at us the government should have continued with its endeavor to see growth in exports at the level which was achieved over a continuous period of ten long years. The Government's inability to react to economic and market indicators and trends and come up with course corrections in respect of policy interventions, particularly in respect of exchange rate, has caused this sharp decline in exports. Considering that most of our exports are price sensitive and we do not respond to drop in world prices, we lost out on exports. The government of the day should be held accountable for this avoidable disaster. Also, it was incumbent upon the think tanks and research organisations to initiate a public debate and sensitise the government about the emerging economic trends. The fallout of the decline in exports has had repercussions not only on GDP but also on employment, hunger, malnutrition, healthcare, education, etc.

Exports have to be given an extra impetus to add to the overall demand and improve the scale of operations to become globally competitive. Additional fillip for increasing exports should start immediately. India's growth has largely been dependent on domestic consumption. In the last two decades our domestic consumption has been increasing due to increasing number of middle class households. The recent trend which shows no growth (or very little growth) in employment is, indeed, very worrying. This is likely to cause stagnation in the size of our middle class and would consequently result in reduced growth in internal consumption which, in turn, would cause reduction in the GDP growth. As reported by CMIE, 11 million jobs (9.1 rural and 1.8 urban) were lost in the year 2018 and this ought to be a cause of concern for the government.

With this trend continuing, there is an urgent need for immediate action to reverse it as otherwise even a 5 to 6 per cent growth in GDP may become difficult to achieve. If that happens, it would consign a large part of our population into perpetual poverty. To reverse this possibility, many steps are required. These are: a) to increase exports to a level at which they account for 20 to 25 per cent of the GDP; b) currency value to be allowed to drop immediately to make Indian products and services competitive—this will help increase exports immediately; c) modification of labour laws to keep employees who started working after a cut-off date out of the prevailing labour law regime; d) encouraging the use of labour in place of expensive capital equipment; and e) wages of regular workers and those employed on casual basis should not be very different, and casual employment should be discouraged.

The argument that our exports suffered due to sluggish international trade is baseless. The real reason is we have not remained price competitive. Correction of exchange rate would have solved the problem and even if it is done now, it can provide some fillip to exports.

The MSME (Micro, Small and Medium Enterprises) sector is the second largest employer in India, next only to agriculture. It employs over 110 million[60] workmen in a variety of activities such as gems and jewellery, food processing, packaging, chemicals, carpet weaving, services (including IT), apparels, textiles, etc. This sector has over 63 million units and is reported to be making over 6,000 products.[61] It has capital assets of over Rs 15 lac crores and accounts for about 25 per cent of the country's GDP.[62] It accounts for 45 per cent of total exports.[63] Almost 95 per cent of the units in this sector continue to remain informal. This sector has had major setbacks as a result of demonetization and the poorly planned roll out of Goods and Services Tax (GST). Informal MSMEs are really very small in size and operations; these are owner driven enterprises and managed through very small transactions, a lot of these done in cash. Most of these enterprises were caught totally unawares by the announcement of demonetizing 86 per cent of the currency in circulation. The buyers as well as the suppliers were left with no currency to transact. There are some estimates that indicate that about 25 per cent of the total MSMEs went bankrupt and closed shop.

It is not just the MSMEs that suffered sudden loss of revenue/ business. The whole chain of economic activity connected with these MSMEs came to a standstill due to their closure. Most reports indicate that a lot of MSMEs have not come back to their original number even after two years. Not long after demonetization, government introduced GST. Once again, it is these MSMEs that suffered the most because of their lack of preparedness to follow the GST guidelines. It appears that 60 per cent of these enterprises were outside the tax net earlier and were not used to filing any compliance documentation. They did not have the wherewithal to hire professional services to help them with the new GST regulations. Penalties for non-compliance being high, some of them had to wind up their establishments. Some of those into exports were not able to continue because refunds of duty drawbacks stopped from the government for quite a while. They were starved of working capital and were unable to continue with their businesses. As per the Economic Survey 2016-17, the estimated loss due to demonetization to GDP is estimated to be around 1 per cent.[64]

Loss of GDP arising because of inability to comply with GST requirements is yet not estimated or known. MSMEs, which are a large contributor to the economy and employment, were assumed to be capable to handle the onslaught of demonetization and the complicated GST; this proved to be completely wrong. It reflected a complete disconnect on the part of the government with the capability and concerns of the MSME sector.

In the last couple of years (from early 2017), credit off-take from the banking system by MSMEs has dropped from 17 per cent to below 14 per cent and the decline is continuing.[65] This explains the plight of this sector. According to the Reserve Bank of India, their creditworthiness has deteriorated in this period and, hence, there is a problem of providing more credit to them. Whatever the issues, this sector is much too important for our country to be left to its own devices. India has a unique dependence on this sector—25 per cent of GDP.[66] Among the developed countries, Italy has a large, small and medium enterprise sector which contributed substantially to their GDP—20.8 per cent in 2017;[67] this is lower than India. China's small and medium sectors contribute 60 per cent of their GDP.[68] Out of proportion growth in the number of units in this sector is largely due to impractical laws, regulations and bureaucratic hassles as otherwise it is not normal to have this sort of skewed development. There are a lot of owners running multiple MSMEs from a single premises on paper. They are unwilling to amalgamate because of stringent compliance requirements. Even our tax laws discourage amalgamation of small and inefficient establishments. Our labour laws are also a very big impediment to making small firms bigger to become efficient.

So, what we need to do is to:

a) Simplify procedures and incentivise owners to register their firms (by providing tax rebate for every person employed by them). Instead of giving concessions on taxes and duties based on turnover, we should consider giving concessions based on number of people employed by them. This would help enterprises to grow their scale of operation;
b) Simplify procedures and reduce the number of required compliances;
c) Urgently amend labour laws;
d) Provide monitory incentives for innovation and growth;
e) Remove all incentives that encourage these establishments to remain small; and
f) Help manufacturing industry in every possible way to improve its productivity.

India's agriculture sector is the backbone of the economy and yet the people involved in this sector are a deprived lot perpetually concerned about their future. This sector is extremely labour intensive, heavily manned, and with no appetite for additional manpower. Agriculture and the allied sectors are the largest source of livelihood in India. About 70 per cent of the rural households still depend upon agriculture for their livelihood.[69] India is the largest producer of food grains in the world accounting for about 25 per cent of the world output.[70] In addition, India produced about 176.4 million tonnes of milk in 2017-18.[71] It is the second largest producer in the world next only to USA. While these statistics look very heartening and should reflect the well-being of farmers and people employed in this activity, the situation on the ground is just the opposite. With increase in population, land holding per household has decreased and this phenomenon has increased the number of dependents per unit of land holding. The farm sector in India employs 53 per cent of the working population and contributes only 17 per cent of our GDP.[72] The government gives many types of subsidies to the farmers (cultivators) in the form of free electricity and water, subsidised fertilizers, frequent loan waivers, the latest being grants to small land holders (12.5 crore of our farmers have small holdings and will become entitled to this grant).[73]

It is strange that no thought has been given to farm labour who outnumber farmers in the ratio of 1:1.25. Agricultural labour is the most exploited unorganised class of rural population and this has its roots in the 'Zamindaari' system. In some areas of the country, bonded labour still continues to exist despite the fact that it has been legally banned. Availability of cheap labour is the single most significant reason for our very poor farm productivity. Indian agricultural sector employs four times the number of people per unit tonne of produce in comparison to the world average.[74] If we were to incentivise improvement in productivity, there would be a reduction in manpower requirement. But, ironically, there are no other employment opportunities available for them. This is how we have caused stress in the farm sector. This stress cannot be removed if over 50 per cent of our total population continues to depend upon a sector that contributes just 17 per cent to the GDP. The population of people dependent on agriculture has to come down by about 50 per cent as this is the only way to reduce the stress on this sector.

The two questions that need to be addressed are:

a) How to physically achieve this; and
b) Since improvement in farm productivity will render a lot of people surplus, we have to have options for their utilisation.

The first thing to do is to make the use of the farm labour expensive by increasing minimum wages to a level at which they do not fall below the defined poverty line. This will also work towards eradicating the propensity of the farm labour to remain poor. Also, farmers should be encouraged to think of farm mechanisation as an alternative to improve their productivity. Employment of labour rendered surplus has been discussed in detail under opportunities for employment in India.

Some facts about child labour in India are as follows:

a) As per the Census of 2011, India had an unbelievable number of over 10.1 million children in the age group of 5-14 working as child labour;[75]
b) About 80 per cent of child labour in India is in rural areas.[76] These children get pulled in primarily due to poverty;
c) Agriculture and cultivation account for over 60 per cent of child labour;[77]
d) UP employed the highest number of child labour in the country.[78] UP has the highest population of children;
e) Our country acknowledges the right of children in the age group of 6 to 14 to free and compulsory education

under the Right to Education Act (RTE) under Article 21a of the Constitution. This leaves children between the ages of 14 to 18 outside the legal purview of the RTE. This must be modified to enable children to complete their education up to Class 10. This perhaps is the reason for a very large number of children in the age group of 15 to 18 years working as child labour;

f) India is sadly the largest employer of child labour in the world. A census revealed an increase in the number of child labour from around 11.3 million in 1991 to 12.7 million in 2001.[79] Nearly half a million children, out of which about 200,000 are below 14, toil for 8 to 12 hours a day in cotton seed production industry. These children who are exposed to poisonous pesticides are mostly school dropouts from Dalits, Adivasis and from Backward Castes while around 70 per cent are trafficked from other states:[80]

g) It is very common to see children employed as domestic helps working for their masters for over 12 hours a day for very low wages. They survive on leftover food and abysmal living conditions; and

h) The Child Labour (Prohibition and Regulation) Act of 1986 prohibits employment of children below the age of 14 years in hazardous occupations. The list of such hazardous jobs was expanded in 2006 and again in 2008 prohibiting employment of children in 18 occupations and 65 processes that are considered hazardous to children's lives and health.

Our legal framework has sufficient depth and breadth to

protect children being used as labour; still we have rampant use of child labour even in occupations that are not supposed to be using child labour. Most common violators are to be found in carpet weaving, cracker making and selling, cinder picking, catering at railway stations, foundries, etc. (the list is very long). Authorities are unable to stop children being employed and exploited in these occupations as long as there is extreme poverty prevailing in the country. Now foreign carpet buyers insist on sellers certifying that weavers have not used child labour in making of carpets being sold by them. While everyone in the chain agrees that children should not be made to work, it is the extreme poverty of the family that forces them to make their children work and earn whatever money they can. Otherwise they would be left to starve. Unless we solve the problem of extreme poverty in our country, it is not going to be possible to get rid of child labour.

To deprive children of their childhood joys is nothing short of a criminal offence. These children grow up with distorted minds with some even taking to crime as their occupation. There is nothing more important for the nation than to solve this problem—a very complex issue that would require concerted efforts at legislative as well as bureaucratic levels at the Centre as well as the States. In addition, it would require a lot of engagement of institutions and NGOs with the stakeholders to sensitise them to the issue as the vested interest groups would like this wretched practice to continue. Albert Einstein said, "The world is a dangerous place to live; not because of the people who are evil, but because of the people who don't do anything about it." It is time that public groups and activists put pressure on the exploiters as well as the government to get rid of this practice. This problem can be eradicated only by making sure that extreme poverty is eradicated from all pockets in the country. How to do that is the subject at hand.

Women should be encouraged to take up jobs. Educating more women and treating them as equals is essential for our economic development. It thus becomes necessary to have similar conditions of employment for men and women. A recent amendment to increase maternity leave has caused a lot of harm to their employment opportunities. Employers have, in fact, reduced recruitment of women drastically. Recent employment statistics show a definite decline in their recruitment. This must be corrected. We could even consider the possibility of some incentives for employers to recruit more women. Employed women, in addition to managing the household properly, play a significant and supportive role in the education of children and partnering in meeting other social obligations.

To increase jobs universally, the government could consider giving incentives to employers in the form of reduced corporate tax based on the number of people employed. In the meantime, the Central as well as the State Governments should fill up all their vacancies. It requires some political will and a bureaucratic shake-up to see that these vacancies are filled up as early as possible.

According to the last report on the subject tabled by our Central Home Ministry in the Lok Sabha on 26 July 2016, India, as on1 January 2015, was short of more than 500,000 police personnel. Consequently, 90 per cent of the police force works for more than eight hours a day. According to another report published in 2014 by Bureau of Police Research and

Development, 68 per cent of the police reported working for 11 hours a day and 28 per cent reported working for 14 hours a day. Nearly half of them reported that they were called for duty between eight to ten times a month while they were off-duty. One learns that our policemen never celebrate festivals with their families. Half a million shortage is with respect to sanctioned strength. From the following table it clearly emerges that our sanctioned force is in itself not sufficient for proper enforcement of law and order in comparison with other countries. Police force per 100,000 of population in different countries is as follows.[81]

USA	207
UK	226
Germany	300
India	150

It cannot be assumed that India needs fewer people for law enforcement than other countries. India, on the contrary, needs a higher strength of police force. One of the factors is that, unlike other countries, we have a very large number of VIPs and VVIPs who require personal protection. The so called VIP and VVIP politicians refuse to be treated as common citizens and are afraid of the very people who have elected them. When VIPs and VVIPs travel through cities, police have to make what they call 'bandobast' lest they get attacked or held up. A large part of the force gets utilised for such duties on a regular basis. Also, there are a disproportionately large number of policemen used for traffic management which is not the case in any developed country.

Maintaining law and order is very important not just to keep the crime rate low but to also attract industry and investments. No one is prepared to invest at a place where one is not assured of the safety of its people and assets. Bihar is a glaring example. It is one of our larger states in area as well as population and yet, is one of the least industrialised. It is also one of our poorer states in terms of per capita income. Against the sanctioned strength of about 1.28 lac policemen, according to figures available, it has only around 78,000 personnel.[82] Bihar is only a case in point but there are a number of states similarly placed.

To make people feel that they are part of a civilized nation, we must strengthen our law enforcement agencies immediately. Here we have a great opportunity for creating employment. No time should be lost in filling up the available half a million vacancies. We should also consider increasing the numbers in the police force from the present 150 to at least 200 per 100,000 population. This will go a long way in creating a secure environment for attracting investment for sustained growth.

The Armed Forces Special Power Act (AFSPA) should be withdrawn from J&K and North East. It is doing more harm than good. The army is trained to fight and kill the enemy and not maintain law and order within the country. By using armed forces for dealing with our own people we are softening their approach and mindset. When it comes to dealing with one's own people, police is the best agency. What we really need to do is to recruit local youngsters and train them adequately for the job of policing. At the same time, we should increase their presence by increasing their strength to between 350 to 400 policemen for every 100,000 population in these troubled areas.

The Russians were not able solve their problem in Chechnya by deploying the military. They failed miserably in their attempts to subjugate the population through brute military force. Ultimately, they solved the problem by local policing.

Travel and tourism is another very important economic sector from the point of view of employment. According to World Travel & Tourism Council (WTTC), it creates jobs and generates prosperity across the world. In their annual analysis of its global economic impact, the sector accounts for 10.4 per cent of global GDP and 313 million jobs or 9.9 per cent of total employment. The year 2017 was one of the strongest years of GDP growth of the decade with robust worldwide consumer spending. In the recent years, performance was particularly strong across Asia. Travel and tourism, which already supports one in every ten jobs on the planet, is a powerful engine for creating employment opportunities. Since India attracts tourists from all parts of the world, the government must take a holistic approach and get all the stakeholders to work with a defined focus to put together packages that would help tourism grow. It is estimated that if tourism was handled a little more imaginatively and given the required support, nearly 100 million new jobs could be created in a decade. This estimate is neither optimistic nor exaggerated.

Travel and tourism contributed nearly Rs 15,240 billion (USD 240 billion) to our country's GDP in the year 2018. The sector directly supported over 42.6 million jobs, which is 8.1 per cent of the total employment in India.[83] Besides the direct revenue generated, the sector also accounted for 5.4 per cent of the total exports as visitor merchandise exports.[84]

In the year 2018, India had 10.5 million tourist arrivals from various countries.[85] Thailand recorded 38.3 million, Malaysia 25.8 million and Singapore 14.7 million.[86] India received close to one-fourth the number of tourists compared to Thailand. Considering the size of our country, its cultural diversity, its coastline, its history and its culinary diversity, we seem to have just about scratched the surface of our potential in travel, tourism and hospitality. If unemployment is our fundamental problem, we must make all-out efforts to attract more and more tourists into the country. Most people attribute our failure in this area to our very bureaucratic way of solving the problems that tourists face while travelling into and within the country. The process of immigration at airports has improved a lot in the recent past. Air travel within India has also become comfortable. Tourists do not seem to have problems on these counts. However, the last mile connectivity to tourist spots/sites continues to remain a serious problem even today. A lot is needed to be done on the quality of road transport in respect of quality of coaches and punctuality of service. Most international tourists avoid travelling by trains in India because of the unhygienic conditions. Our railway stations are rated as the most unfriendly in the world. Most tourists, particularly the elderly, tend to avoid railway stations because of the inconvenience experienced by them.

Tourists, as a rule, travel to other countries primarily for enjoyment. They look for relaxation and indulge in activities that they enjoy most. Visiting historical places and those that provide an insight into a different culture is only an additional attraction. Most people, after exploring different places like to revisit a resort for a holiday that provides good recreation facilities. Such facilities are very scarce in our country. If we have to attract tourists and get them to spend their summer vacations in July/August (vacation months in Europe), we have to get a little more innovative and make our monsoon season attractive. We should attract tourists by providing facilities of indoor games such as billiards, badminton, table tennis, indoor swimming, card rooms and even casinos. Small stake gambling in casinos, along with other recreational facilities, will go a long way in attracting tourists from Europe. Ideally, these centers should have direct flights. During the winter months, particularly in December/January, we get a substantial number of foreign tourists. Hotels in Goa, Kerala and a few other places which are popular tourist destinations use the supply shortage condition for increasing their tariffs steeply—sometime double or even treble. This has a huge impact on the perception creation with the tourists. A lot of tourists drop out on knowing the abnormally high tariffs. It defies all logic that a country as large as India should have only a few winter destinations.

The United Nations recognises the potential of tourism in the development agenda of the world. In 2018, the Asia Pacific Region, Europe and Americas received 284, 464 and 296 million tourists respectively.[87] Tourism has promoted regional and sub-regional cooperation and is a key feature of overall economic integration and sustainable development agenda in the world and the Asia Pacific Region. This region alone accounted for about 30 per cent of world tourism.[88]

With the serious unemployment problem that we have in India, the development and nurturing of this sector assumes very high importance. India should seriously work towards doubling its tourist footfalls in the next few years. It is estimated that 40 million additional jobs could be created if we were to double our tourist arrivals. Considering the additional foreign exchange that this sector gets, it becomes even more valuable.

Some suggestions towards this objective are:

a) Reduce the currency value to make India, cost wise, a more attractive tourist destination;
b) Create more beach resorts along our long coastline. These resorts should be equipped with all the state of the art recreational facilities that cater to tourists of all age groups;
c) Such resorts could also be located near large inland water bodies. Foreign tourists who have visited Tungabhadra Dam have enjoyed the scenic beauty around this dam;
d) Shed inhibitions and fears about casinos. People have a natural instinct to gamble. Small-time gambling provides a great level of recreation. We allow betting on horse races, on stock exchanges (in shares as well as commodities), so there is no reason to have a problem with casinos. Most countries have legalised gambling. Legalising it is a better option than to let the activity thrive in the hands of people who operate the underworld. It would generate employment and would be a huge attraction and an additional source of revenue for the government;
e) Atlantic City (USA), which is located south of New York, is visited by millions of rich people. Casinos are the primary attraction of the city. There are a large number of casinos on the city's beach front and these are busy round the clock, seven days a week. While

casinos are the primary attraction, the city has some of the finest theaters, restaurants, cinemas, skating rinks, beside the beautiful beach that the city offers. This city provides unforgettable short duration holidays. Our eastern coast has quite a few beautiful beaches and we can easily create many Indian versions of the Atlantic City along it;

f) Clean up the areas surrounding cultural sites and encourage multi-cuisine restaurants in the vicinity. Approach to these sites should be clean and should be designed in a manner in which it generates curiosity about the place; and
g) Improve the rail and road transport system to a level at which moving through cities to places of attraction becomes a worthwhile experience.

This is only a small wish list that clearly indicates that a lot needs to be done to attract more tourists into the country. It is time that the Ministry of Tourism is given the importance it deserves and some of the smarter and market savvy bureaucrats are posted there. It would also be a good idea to get some experts from the best tourist destinations such as Thailand to advise the ministry on how to make the country more tourist friendly.

We ought to work on tourism with an objective of increasing the inflow of tourists by 25 per cent per annum. It is a huge challenge but with the potential India has to offer, it certainly is achievable. Taxes on hotel tariffs and food should be reduced. This will reduce revenue collection marginally, and that too for a short period, but would increase tourist footfalls which will eventually improve gross revenue collection for the country. Most importantly, it will create huge employment opportunities.

A very popular song *What a wonderful world* sung by a famous singer, Louis Daniel Armstrong, describes the world as wonderful with green trees, colourful roses, etc. It is an American singing about America. In America, 60 per cent of the poor have cars and air conditioners. If he were an Indian, he would have probably sung *What a wretched world* and described people with empty stomachs, begging bowls in their hands and misty eyes walking aimlessly not knowing where to head. Indian poverty is quite different compared to that in America. Jawaharlal Nehru in his book, *Discovery of India*, opined that "there was lack of food, clothing, housing and every other essential requirement of human existence. The development policy objective should be to get rid of the appalling poverty of people".

We have strayed away from our main objectives. In mid 90s we changed over from socialistic to capitalistic economy. Like fanatics, we adopted the American way of pure capitalism. We perceived socialism and capitalism as the only two options available for economic management as if there was nothing in between. Many European countries (particularly Scandinavia), very successfully followed the middle path of capitalism with socialist leaning. India, with over 50 per cent of its people being poor, cannot afford to completely ignore this part of the population. What we have done is unethical and immoral. This blind approach has landed us in a situation that has resulted in huge disparity in income and wealth in our society. According to current reckoning, 1 per cent of Indians own 73 per cent of the country's wealth.[89] The disparity is higher than the most capitalist countries such as USA and Germany, our role models. And, this disparity keeps growing with time. It is not a sign of a thriving economy but a symptom of a failing economic system. Let us not forget that those working hard to grow food for the nation, building its infrastructure, and working in factories are struggling to fund their children's education, buy medicines and even manage two meals a day.

The assumption that if we create wealth in the country, the trickle-down effect will remove poverty has not materialised; in fact, it has been proved wrong. Very low wages and transfer of natural resources cheaply to the rich has in reality resulted in creating more poverty. As discussed earlier, if we were to have male participation in the workforce equal to China of 68 per cent, we have about 50 million additional people for employment (the difference in male labour participation ratio of China and India). Female labour participation in our country currently is only 23.3 per cent.[90] Low participation has its roots in tradition and lack of opportunities. If female participation were to increase to 40 per cent (possible level to achieve in the next 10 years), we have another 60 million employable women looking for jobs. For employing women, we may have to incentivise employers suitably. Creating opportunities for employing additional 50 million males and 60 million females to our workforce is indeed a very daunting and challenging task.

About 42 per cent[91] of the employed work for the agriculture and allied sectors and generate just about 15.2 per cent of our GDP.[92] This level of dependence on this sector is just not sustainable. Our focus has to shift to mechanising of farming to reduce the number of people dependent on agriculture for survival. Currently nearly 170 million people are employed in this activity. In order to double the farmers' income we need to reduce the current workforce by half to double the output per person. Our present government's promise of doubling farmers' income can be met only through increasing productivity by mechanisation. This would mean creating additional job opportunities for approximately 85 million people, in addition to the 110 million discussed in the preceding paragraphs.

This requires a radical out of the box thinking. To begin with we must understand that GDP is sum total of consumption of every citizen of the country. Every human is a source of consumption and, therefore, a contributor to GDP.

Allowing foreign investment in retail was a serious mistake on the part of the government. It will neither benefit the seller nor the buyer. It will not help the economy of the country but only cause massive unemployment. This is particularly true for retailers of grocery. Our *kirana* shops currently provide very satisfactory service and employ millions, most of whom will become jobless gradually. This process will only transfer wealth from the poor to the wealthy and increase the disparity even more. Retailing by corporate houses is beneficial only in countries that are short of workforce and not for a poor country like India where people are starving because of lack of employment.

Gross Domestic Product (GDP) or Gross Value Addition (GVA) represents Consumption (domestic) + Governmental expenditure + Investments + (exports – imports). In short GDP/GVA represents a country's overall consumption plus net exports.

The overall consumption of a country is a function of

essentially the size of its middle class (number of rich people being small, their aggregate consumption is low). The poor, on the other hand, consume very little because they have no money. In developed countries, the size of middle class remains more or less stable. This class does not go through significant annual growth and, hence, the GDP growth in these countries remains stable but moderate. Most developed countries show an annual growth of 2 to 3 per cent. Growth in excess of this is considered very healthy. In some developed countries, where induction of educated immigrants is part of country's policy, the size of middle class keeps increasing through immigration. Consumption caused by new entrants helps in increasing the GDP. USA has benefitted a great deal by this policy which is likely to continue in the foreseeable future as well. Because of this policy, USA will always have higher GDP growth than most other developed countries.

Our growth story has suffered quite a few setbacks in the last few years. Not only has the size of our middle class stopped growing, our exports have registered negative growth rate in the past four years. Whatever growth in GDP/GVA that we now see is due to lower middle class migrating to middle class. It is commendable that we clocked 7.2 per cent annual GDP growth in 2017-18.[93] This is likely to go down as a significant part of our GDP is a function of the annual growth in the size of our middle class and the increase in our exports. Both these factors are currently in negative zone and require urgent attention if we have to keep the growth clock ticking. Increase in the size of middle class is directly related to the creation of new employment opportunities. People who get jobs must be adequately compensated so that they get into lower middle class and become consumers. Tackling negative growth in exports is comparatively easy because it requires adequate devaluation of the currency to ensure that Indian products become competitive again in the international markets. The fear that a cheaper rupee will increase our dollar dominated oil imports and would widen our current account deficit is not logical. Higher exports will benefit us in getting higher inflow of foreign currency to more than offset the increase in cost of importing oil and other goods. If we had continued with 15 per cent growth in exports, we would have had additional exports of over USD 200 billion clocking additional GDP by the same amount in the current year alone.

The Wire headline says—Richest 1% cornered 73% Wealth Generated in India in 2017: Oxfam Survey.[94] In the period between 1993-94 and 2011-12, ordinary workers saw their income rise by an average of just 3.7 per cent a year.[95] While there were only 9 billionaires in 2000, the number increased to 101 in 2017.[96] The wealth of billionaires increased tenfold in a decade and it was more than the total Union Budget for 2018-19.[97-98]

Over the years, we have facilitated rich people becoming richer and poor becoming poorer. Expected trickle-down effect has actually not happened. Hard working labour has actually been subsidising the rich. As a rule, companies should not be allowed to pay high salaries to executives unless the lowest paid workmen are paid wages that would enable them to live comfortably. Even the payment of dividend or the bonus shares to shareholders should be subjected to this criterion. One should also consider limiting executive wages to a given multiple of median wage paid to the workmen. The ratio of salary drawn by the highest paid executive and the lowest paid workmen in some companies works out to 5000:1. Can this difference be justified ethically or morally? In a poor country like India, these questions need an urgent answer. While the decision maker in a corporate is all powerful and decides his own salary the non-unionised workman remains absolutely helpless. People require jobs at whatever wage and working condition they are offered—they don't have the power to bargain. Giving abysmally low salary to people who have been deprived socially and economically for centuries can be corrected only by providing a strong legal framework and simultaneously sensitising the people who are supposed to generate wealth. Asking the corporate sector to spend 2 per cent of their profit for social causes is absolutely meaningless in the current circumstances. This money should go to the State exchequer for better use.

China has managed to remove poverty from its country. Nearly 800 million of her poor people have actively joined the country's mainstream economic activity since 1990.[99] We have, on the other hand, increased our count of poor people in the same period. Ignoring the poor is already proving to be very expensive in economic terms. The situation will become even worse with time. If additional funds are required to tackle this problem, we must find ways and means for generating them. It is possible that we would require additional revenue in the range of Rs 3 to 4 lac crores annually (increasing with time) to run our suggested programmes for the next ten to fifteen years to get rid of poverty from all pockets of the country.

Our national resources like ores, as mentioned earlier, are the property of every citizen of the country. We must assign a certain underlying value to all our natural resources which should be collected as cess at the mining level. With this additional amount along with the budgetary allocation already being made will help MGNREGA to provide jobs to every person who is in need of one without limiting number of days and at proper wages.

Increase in taxes is essential if the condition of the large number of poor is to be alleviated in a reasonable period of time. Corporate tax should be increased by 5 per cent or more if required. We should also do away with the 2 per cent Corporate Social Responsibility burden which, in any case, does not seem to be benefitting the country in any significant manner. This should be abolished and added to the normal corporate tax which would make the tax increase by an additional 7 per cent. It would benefit the country and will improve the employment opportunities. Bringing back our old practice of tax rebate on fresh investments will also help. Attempt should be to collect additional Rs 50,000 to 100,000 crores by these measures. One should have absolutely no doubt that whatever extra wages we pay to the poor will come back to the market many times over as consumption and increase the country's GDP.

Since increasing personal taxes is non-productive, the emphasis should be to collect taxes on expenditure. Some items of use (consumer durables, in particular) which are bought only by the rich are not price sensitive. GST on such items should be much beyond the current highest slab. There is no need to have a limited number of GST rates. The growing class of the rich and their obsession with lifestyle and consumerism should be utilised for collecting additional revenue. We believe that Rs 20,000 to 25,000 crores per year can be generated through this process alone. The future of our country is primarily dependent on the rate of removal of poverty in the country.

SUMMARY OF RECOMMENDATIONS

The principal recommendation is to increase employment leading to increase in consumption of goods and services to alleviate poverty and simultaneously increase GDP. Double digit growth in GDP is easily possible in India if we were to adopt the policy to bring increased number of people into consumption cycle. The objective should be to increase our GDP through consumption and not vice versa.

A. Immediate

a) Fill all vacancies lying vacant in the Government (Central and States).

b) Fill all vacancies in the police force and plan to utilise the police for effective public service.

d) The vacancies in teaching staff in schools and colleges to be filled up and the quality of education imparted to go through an overhaul.

e) Provide tax incentive to private sector that opts for labour vis-a-vis machines.

f) Increase minimum wages for casually employed by 50 per cent irrespective of sector in which employed, including those under MGNREGA.

g) Remove limits on the number of days a person is eligible to be employed under MGNREGA.

h) Remove the 2 per cent CSR obligation of profit making corporate houses. Collect this as a tax.

i) Increase Corporate Tax by 5 per cent.

j) Give rebates for investment and additional employment.
k) High priority needs to be given to increase exports.

B. Medium and Long Term

a) Target an annual increase in the number of tourists visiting India by 15 to 20 per cent.
b) "Make in India" programme needs to be given a hard push to make it successful.
c) Attracting international companies for making India their manufacturing base in preference to China.
d) Labour laws need to be reformed to ensure improved human productivity.
e) Start work in a phased manner on the linking of rivers.

Indian Police Under Captivity

To insure the adoration of a theorem for any length of time, faith is not enough; a police force is needed as well.

—Albert Camus

(Author, Philosopher, Nobel Laureate)

If the police need more help to do their work, I will not hesitate in granting it to them.

—Theresa May

(Former Prime Minister of UK)

IN INDIA, law and order is a State subject so the police have been put under the control of respective governments in the states and union territories. The candidates selected for the State Police Services (SPS) are usually posted as Deputy Superintendent of Police or Assistant Commissioner of Police upon completion of their probation. On satisfactory service in the SPS, a select set of officers are nominated to be a part of the prestigious Indian Police Service (IPS). The structure, responsibilities and duties of the police force are governed by the Indian Police Act (IPA) of 1861 enacted during the British Raj. The Imperial power enacted the IPA as a direct consequence of the revolt of 1857. This Act was essentially to oppress people into submission and to avoid more similar revolts. It was based on the colonial mistrust of the lower ranks of the service. Under this Act, decision making was supposed to lie with the few high placed white Sahibs while the local constables were merely expected to follow orders.

After Independence, there were many voices advocating changes in the system but nothing really happened. Our police system continues to remain almost intact. The white Sahibs have been replaced by brown Sahibs (the elected Chief Ministers and Home Ministers of the states along with the bureaucrats who are a part of their exploitative caucus). The divide between the 'elected' rulers and the common people still remains just as it was in the British Raj.

According to some, this divide has actually increased. It is disturbingly visible when a VIP's motorcade of as many as 15 to 20 cars happens to be passing through a residential area. Roads are cleared of traffic and even ambulances carrying patients are stalled for our brown Sahib to reach his destination without going through the usual hassles that ordinary citizens are subjected to on a regular basis. VIPs travelling by air are hosted in lounges and segregated from all those people who have voted them to these coveted positions. It is ironical that average people are faced with discrimination at the hands of those who are supposed to be working for them.

After Independence, there was a good reason to throw the colonial legacy out of the window and set up a new structure that would make the police force and policing people-friendly and accountable to the people. Unfortunately, that never happened. As years passed, successive governments found it convenient to misuse the police for meeting their own political ends. Through the 1960s many State governments took the initiative of setting up commissions to examine the functioning and problems of the police force. The Government of India also set up a committee on police training in 1971,[1] and later in 1977 the National Police Commission[2] was set up. This Commission was set up by the Janata Party Government in the aftermath of the Emergency that was imposed in 1975. It was entrusted with the task of reviewing the functions of police and the flaws within the existing system of police administration. The commission described the threat of transfers or suspension as the most potent weapon in the hands of the politician to tame the police. This enables them to flout rules and indulge in criminal activities and in white collar crimes without the fear of being apprehended or convicted. The powerful grip on the police force also helps the politicians in power to tame the vocal and inconvenient opposition leadership.

The commission recommended that the powers of the state governments be limited to ensuring that the police operate in strict accordance with the law, thereby circumscribing the broad powers vested with the state governments. Such changes along with assured security of tenure would minimise political interference in the operational performance of the police and encourage greater professionalism in the force. The National Police Commission (NPC) submitted eight detailed reports between 1979 and 1981 with comprehensive recommendations covering the entire gamut of police work. By then the government had changed and so had the priorities. The new dispensation had lost interest in changing the working of the police force which was meant to benefit the public but not generate any advantage for the people in power.

In 1983, when the Central Government forwarded the core recommendations to the States, the response that it received was lukewarm. Nothing really happened. Recommendations were conveniently buried as it is with the recommendations of most of the committees and commissions in India.

The present hierarchical organizational structure of State police force has 13 levels as under:

- Director General of Police
- Special Director General of Police
- Additional Director General of Police
- Inspector General of Police
- Deputy Inspector General of Police
- Senior Superintendent of Police
- Superintendent of Police
- Deputy/Assistant Superintendent of Police
- Inspector
- Sub Inspector
- Assistant Sub Inspector
- Head Constable
- Constable

Senior level positions in the police force are held by officers of all India cadre called the Indian Police Service (IPS). IPS is one of the three All India Services (AIS) which include Indian Administrative Service (IAS), Indian Foreign Service (IFS) and Indian Police Service (IPS). Members of IAS and IPS are recruited by Union Government but they are assigned to various States and Union Territories with the mandate to serve under the State and/or under Central Governments. This is considered one of the important tools that makes the Union Government stronger than State Governments. Officers of these services comply with All India Service Rules relating to pay, conduct, leave, various allowances, etc. Ministry of Home Affairs (Central Government) is the authority for the IPS cadre of police officers.

There are another two channels to acquire IPS cadre. These are:

a) Officers in the State Police Service (SPS) who have secured a good rank and have progressed well in their career can get promoted to IPS after 15-20 years of service; and
b) If one has lower rank in UPSC's Central Services Examination (CSE) and gets selected in Group B Service like DANIPS—which is the police service for Union territories—one may get promoted to IPS after 15-20 years of service.

The Indian Police Service is responsible for internal security, public safety and law and order. In 1948, a year after independence, the Imperial Police (IP) was replaced by the name Indian Police Service (IPS).[3] IPS is not a law enforcement agency in its own right—rather it is the body to which all senior police officers belong regardless of the agency for which they work. They are entrusted with the overall law and order of the entire State as the Director General of Police, the entire District as its Superintendent of Police, and in Metropolitan cities as Deputy Commissioner of Police. As Commissioner of Police, they enjoy magisterial power as well. IPS is the only service which is within striking distance of equality with IAS in terms of powers, authority and speed in promotions.

An IPS officer takes charge as an Assistant Superintendent of Police of a subdivision after his probation of two years. The tenure of this post is normally two years. His next appointment is as Superintendent of Police or Deputy Commissioner. They then get promoted to junior administrative grade in nine years of joining and selection grade in 13 years; then as Deputy Inspector General of Police or Additional Commissioner of Police in 14 years, an Inspector General of Police in 18 years, Additional Director General of Police in 25 years and finally, the Director General of Police after 30 years of service. They also get posted to national agencies such as the Intelligence Bureau, Research and Analysis Wing, Central Bureau of Investigation, etc. Other jobs like Director General of Border Security Force, Central Reserve Police Force, Central Industrial Security Force, etc. are also open to them.

The structure of the force has no doubt been very thoughtfully designed to discharge their functions within the framework of the constitutional provisions. What seems to be missing are the policy guidelines and clearly defined objectives for discharging their functions and their performance to be measured by an independent body, without any conflict of interest. The absence of an independent body to review the performance remains a big flaw in the system. Upright officers who do not give in to the desires of the authority invariably get punished. This of course applies to the IAS cadre as well.

The function of this force is to: a) enforce the law of the land in a non-partisan manner; b) provide protection to people and their property; c) investigate crimes with objectivity and in a non-partisan manner; and d) under no circumstances allow anyone to take the law into their own hands. This is what we, as citizens, expect from the police force. However, the ground realities are very different. There is huge underreporting of crimes by the victims lest they themselves become the accused at the hands of the investigating agencies. A very common phenomenon is that the victim who reports the matter gets booked as the accused and is even punished by the courts of law. People are scared of the man in khaki. A simple thing like reporting an accident is avoided for fear that one would have to spend days visiting the police stations and courts if one is named as an eye witness. The inefficiencies of the justice dispensation system coupled with unfriendly and dehumanised approach of the police ensures that many crimes are not even reported because asking for help or resolution from police is, apparently, like asking for trouble. Despite this being common, a lot of cases do get reported and pursued but for doing that one needs to have the zeal of an activist or the desperation of a person who has nothing more to lose. The average educated, peace-loving, law-abiding citizen avoids going to a police station. This is because the experience that one encounters is that of humiliation and extortion. One has to be a person with 'connections' to be able to get the services (either free or for a nominal fee—in cash or as a favour) of the police.

People who belong to this group of service seekers are either politicians, political hobnobbers or bureaucrats. For the wealthy, it is always available for a fee which is dependent on the perception of the wealth of the person, the severity of the crime committed, the degree of the moral and professional degeneration of the investigating officer, and the compulsion for fund collection that the people in power have generated with the police force. Mob lynching of people on mere suspicion has become a common phenomenon. In such cases, there is obvious evidence of the fact that the investigative work by the police is partisan and is done to please their political masters. It would be unfair to put the complete blame on the police—the masters are more to be blamed. But, the ultimate responsibility must be with the police as it is incumbent upon them to operate within the framework of the Constitution and the laid down laws and not make themselves vulnerable to blackmail and arm-twisting.

The Police Act of 1861 which more or less still governs the IPS gives each State government the powers to establish its own police force. Section 3 of the Act authorises the State governments to exercise superintendence over the police. In our criminal justice system, the police is entrusted the job of investigating crimes. It is supposed to coordinate with the prosecution to collect evidence against the accused. But people in power or those having clout get away with blatant violation of law resulting in direct violation of citizens' rights in the form of unauthorised detention, torture, harassment, fabrication of evidence, malicious prosecution, etc. There are glaring examples from the recent past of the erosion of the rule of law or violation of citizens' rights resulting from political control over the police. Continuing with same British law and, more importantly, the mindset which was essentially enacted to suppress the citizens of a slave nation is nothing short of treachery. The problem of political interference in the work of police and its disastrous consequences on the rule of law in our country are well known. This is despite the fact that many commissions, like the one in the year 1977, were appointed. All reports have recommended independence from political interference of the functioning of police force. Similar recommendations by various NGOs, National Human Rights Commission and Commonwealth Human Rights Initiative have been buried or are collecting dust in archives and store-houses. Amongst the various recommendations was a draft Model Police Act that was to replace the outdated 1861 British Act. Governments have come and gone but none has bothered to remedy the continuing human rights violations being committed even against victims of rape and gang rape. This shameful apathy is beyond comprehension.

In 1996, Prakash Singh, Director General of Police in Uttar Pradesh, after his retirement took it upon himself to personally work towards bringing changes in the working of the police. Having spent his life in the police force and being privy to what was happening, he worked passionately towards his chosen objective. He petitioned the Supreme Court urging for the issue of directions to the Government of India to frame a new Police Act on the lines of the Model Act drafted by the Commission in order to ensure that the police are made accountable essentially and primarily, to the laws of the land and the people.[4] He took the issue to the Supreme Court with the prayer to direct the Central and State governments to address the most glaring gaps and bad practices in the functioning of the police. He further prayed that people could not wait any further for the governments to take suitable steps for reforms and, therefore, the Supreme Court needed to issue appropriate directions for immediate compliance and these directions to be made binding upon the governments.

The Supreme Court referred to the recommendations made by various committees on police reforms and culled four points of reforms. These are:

a) State Security Commissions to be set up at state level;
b) Formulate transparent procedure for appointment of a police chief and desirability of giving him a minimum fixed tenure;
c) Separation of investigation work from law and order; and
d) A new Police Act which should reflect the democratic aspirations of the people.

On the issue of whether the Court must wait for the executive to act upon the recommendations, the Court considered the gravity of the problem, the need to enforce the rule of law, the recommendations by the various committees, the ten-year delay in the disposal of the petition and total uncertainty as to when the police reforms would be introduced. The Supreme Court concluded that ordering of directions was warranted.

It delivered a historic judgment on 22 September 2006 on Prakash Singh versus Union of India instructing the Central and State Governments to comply with a set of seven directives, thereby defining a practical framework to kick-start police reforms. The Court directives sought to achieve two main objectives—functional autonomy for the police through security of tenure, streamlined appointments and transfer process and the creation of a body to enhance accountability of the police. After decades of public pressure, lack of political will and continued poor policing, police reforms seemed to be finally coming. The Supreme Court required the Central

Government as well as all State Governments to comply with the seven directives by 31 December 2006 and to file affidavits of compliance by 3 January 2007.

In its judgement dated 22 September 2006, the Supreme Court:

a) Directed each State Government to establish a State Security Commission and a Police Establishment Board to determine transfers, postings, promotions, etc.;
b) Outlined procedure for selection of Director General of Police;
c) Prescribed minimum two years tenure for police officers; and
d) Directed police departments to differentiate law and order functions from investigation.

The Supreme Court also ordered the creation of a district and state level Police Complaints Authority to deal with complaints against the police. It directed the Central Government to constitute a National Security Commission whose main task was to review the existing measures in order to enhance their effectiveness and focus on ameliorating the conditions of the service. The seven directives issued by the Supreme Court are in two categories—one dealing with functional autonomy and the other seeking to enhance police accountability.

The directives issued are:

Category—1 Functional Autonomy

Directive-1 The State Governments are directed to

constitute a State Security Commission: a) to ensure that the State Government does not exercise unwarranted influence or pressure on the police; b) lay down broad policy guidelines; and c) to evaluate the performance of police.

Directive-2 State Government to ensure that the Director General of Police is appointed through a merit based, transparent process and that he enjoys a minimum tenure of two years.

Directive-3 The State Government to ensure that other police officers on operational duties (including Superintendents of Police in charge of a district and Station House Officers in charge of a police station) also have a minimum tenure of two years.

Directive-4 The State Governments to set up Police Establishment Boards which would review all transfers, promotions and other service related matters of police officers of and below the rank of Deputy Superintendent of Police; and make recommendations on postings and transfers of officers above the rank of Deputy Superintendent of Police.

Directive-5 The Central Government to set up a National Security Commission at the Union level to prepare a panel for selection and placement of chiefs of the Central Police Organisations (CPO), who should be given a given a minimum tenure of two years.

Category—2 Accountability Directive

Directive-6 The State Governments to set up independent Police Complaint Authorities at the State and District levels to look into public complaints against police officers in cases of serious misconduct, including custodial death, grievous hurt or rape in police custody.

Directive-7 The State Government is to separate the investigation and law and order functions of the police.

Even while Prakash Singh's Public Interest Litigation (PIL) was pending with Supreme Court, three committees were constituted by the Central Government to look at the need to reform the functioning and administrative structure of the police force. These were a) Ribeiro Committee in 1989; b) Padmanabhan Committee in 2000; and c) Malimath Committee in 2002. All the three committees were of the view that there was an urgent need for reforms with each giving their own recommendations on the need and the type of changes required. Recommendations, though made individually by the committees, were similar in nature. There was complete unanimity in their views in respect of recommending: a) autonomy in the functioning of the force; b) unbiased administrative control on the force; and c) separation of investigation and law and order functions. There was yet another committee—'Soli Sorabjee Committee'—which even drafted a new Model Police Act to replace the Police Act of 1861, and submitted the same to the government on 30 October 2006.The Supreme Court and Sorabjee Committee had very similar views on the reforms. The Supreme Court's judgment came as a relief to the people at large and to various bodies who were fighting for the cause all this while, believing that the long standing problem of police reforms had finally come to an end with a satisfactory outcome. Everyone, obviously, underestimated the resolve of the lobby of politicians and bureaucrats and their ingenuity to subvert even the Supreme Court directives. It is over 14 years since the historic judgement was pronounced but it has had absolutely no effect in the way these people have been operating. In fact, the situation on the ground has worsened. With governments having decided not to implement the reforms and the Supreme Court also, surprisingly, having shown its inability to enforce its directives and with no other higher court to go to for help, the situation is back to square one.

The Supreme Court in its judgement had directed the governments (Central and State) to comply with the directives and provide compliance reports. Response from various State Governments covered the full spectrum—total rejection to compliance. Most of the states, particularly the larger ones, expressed strong objections to the directives and requested the Court to review the orders. Some states requested the Court to grant them more time to comply with the directives. The Supreme Court in response to the various requests rejected all the pleas in its order of 10 January 2007 while directing the States to comply with the directives without any modification.

Some States even questioned the Supreme Court's directives by raising the fundamental premise—'Does the working of the police force need reforms?' According to them, political interference in the police administration was minimal. In raising this fundamental question, they junked all the reports and their recommendations made by various commissions/committees appointed by the government, including reports by various NGOs and Human Rights Commission. Some concluded that setting up State Security Commissions would undermine the powers of the states given to them by the Constitution. According to them, it would reduce the accountability of the police to the people. This claim happens to be just the opposite of the reforms directed by the Supreme Court. They, in a way, questioned the very idea of having independent regulatory bodies like RBI, SEBI, TRAI, etc. Some states also questioned the purpose of Police Establishment Boards. This, they felt was contrary to democratic functioning of the government and would, in their opinion, create a separate power centre. A lot of meaningless objections seem to have been raised just for the sake of delaying the implementation of the directives. Some other states said that they did not believe in giving fixed tenure to DGPs. They felt a fixed tenure was not important for good functioning. The argument given was that fixed tenure would block promotion for the next in the queue. This argument is baseless and without any merit or logic. If a DGP gets two years tenure, his successor will also enjoy two years even if his promotion gets slightly delayed. Politicians themselves enjoy five year tenures in office but are not willing to mandate a two year term to the police chief. Loss of power to transfer, which they use mercilessly as a tool for making police officers subservient, is their real fear. Most states have also shown resistance to establishing a Complaints Authority. The argument that the police will get demoralised is absurd. It means that no one has the right to register a complaint against the police if he/she has been wronged. Lack of concern for the people is the real reason for not wanting to have a Complaints Authority.

Towards the actual implementation of the Supreme Court's directives, 17 states promulgated new acts and 12 others have issued executive orders. New acts or the executive orders issued are meant to circumvent the Supreme Court directives rather than to implement them. The answer to why a new Police Act has not been enacted is, indeed, very simple. Politicians who become ministers exercise their authority through the secretaries in their respective ministries (IAS cadre bureaucrats). This makes the concerned bureaucrat also very powerful. Not only do most bureaucrats enjoy this authority but they also feel superior to the Police Chief who is, theoretically, of the same status as the secretary in the Central Services hierarchy. IAS and IPS have an age-old rivalry running between them. There is yet another reason. Politicians and bureaucrats have a very strong nexus when it comes to subverting the system. Bureaucrats are the ones who have the entire professional wherewithal to run the ministries which most politicians do not possess. A lot of ministers depend solely on their bureaucrats. And, in return, bureaucrats depend on their political bosses for their annual performance appraisals which are very important for IAS cadre officers for their promotions and desired placement. Subversion of Supreme Court's directives has become a common agenda with both the politicians and the bureaucrats. Politicians have found bureaucrats ready to help them in defying the directives. In this process, not only the politicians but the bureaucrats as well have retained their power over the police. Bureaucrats derive vicarious pleasure in showing their power over police in respect of administrative matters.

If the directions of the Supreme Court are blatantly ignored, we have a serious problem in operating as a healthy and functional democracy. Executive and political dispensations that make the Supreme Court a toothless institution is a grave concern. The Economist Intelligence Unit (EIU) published its 11th report on State of Democracies in the world in 2018 titled *Me Too? Political Participation, Protest and Democracy.* The EIU has over seven decades of experience in studying the spectrum of democracies in the world. The report made news last year when India slipped from 32 to 42 in ranking—disgracefully below Latvia and South Africa. This is a comprehensive survey and divides the countries into four categories: a) Full Democracies, b) Flawed Democracies, c) Hybrid Democracies, and d) Authoritarian Regimes. India is categorised as a Flawed Democracy in the latest report. India, which had reached its highest ever position of 27 in 2014, (just two ranks away from Full Democracies), slipped down to 42 in 2018. One of the important reasons for this is denial of equal rights to all citizens of the country, biased investigations, tutored witnesses, lapses in investigations, delayed investigations, etc. which result in discrimination between citizens of differing financial status, religious practices and castes, invariably resulting in miscarriage of justice. As long as our police force remains captive to politicians, we are, and will remain a flawed democracy. But of course, this does not worry our people in power. India's ranking slipped down further 9 ranks to 51 in 2019.

The subject of police reforms seems to have been shelved. People are thrown in jail for crimes they have not committed. Our jails are overflowing with thousands of innocent undertrials languishing for years. Once jailed, society discards them as convicts and with time, they become faceless. The accused continue to remain in jail for unbelievably long periods while trial proceedings keep crawling for years. They are not able to obtain bail, even when entitled to, because of their poor financial condition. Why should a poor man who has no money to provide a bond for his bail remain behind bars if the authorities are unable to convict or even chargesheet him? Such accused are also unable to obtain proper legal help. These faceless accused keep suffering in darkness and hopelessness. The tragedy gets compounded when the accused is innocent. The horrors faced by such people when thrown in jail for crimes they have not committed are incomprehensible. Our country has one of the largest number of imprisoned undertrials languishing in jails. According to the report *Prison Statistics India 2018*, 69.4 per cent (3,23,537) accused are in jails because the authorities have failed to complete their task of determining if the accused is a criminal. This highlights the flawed justice system in India. Why should these poor people be left to rot in jails if the police have not completed their investigation or the transport was not available to escort the accused to the court on the appointed date; or the accused was produced in the court but the presiding judge went on leave; or the accused was produced in court but his case was not taken up on the day? These are but a few examples of how the accused are made to suffer in jails for absolutely no fault of theirs. There are undertrials who have been in jail for over five years without being chargesheeted for a crime they are accused of having committed.

There is a need for people to introspect on the direction that our country and our society has taken in the last few decades—a direction that lacks morality and ethics and the desire to be fair and work towards creating a just society.

The Supreme Court had to once again step in on the report put together by National Legal Services Authority of India

(NALSA) observing that the undertrials who had eligibility to be released on the bases of their illness and mental ill-health had not been released. A division bench of Justice Madan B Lokur and Justice Deepak Gupta, on 10 October 2017, expressed shock and concern as to why such undertrials were not released by the states despite the apex court's earlier direction to them to do so. The bench asked the governments of Uttar Pradesh, Maharashtra, and Madhya Pradesh to submit affidavits on the number of category-wise undertrial prisoners languishing in their prisons and why they were not released, if eligible. They expressed that they would be compelled to seek personal presence of chief secretaries of these states if these affidavits were not filed by 26 October 2017. The court brought to the attention of Attorney General K K Venugopal the report made by NALSA and asked,"What action is the government of India planning to take?" They said that they had already issued necessary directions and yet the Centre was not taking any steps for releasing the eligible undertrials. "Is it not shocking?" the bench questioned. The bench was further shocked by the submission of the Attorney General who said that the Centre had been issuing advisories to the states from time to time to release such prisoners but they were not doing so. He further added that the Centre could only issue an advisory, but had no powers under the Constitution to issue directions to the States. It is for the Supreme Court to direct the States to release the undertrial prisoners, as recommended by the undertrial committee of NALSA. The situation, the bench felt, was very strange. If the advisories by the Centre were not being implemented by the states and were being completely ignored, the Centre should not be issuing advisories. The Centre, the bench observed, could not plead helplessness. This exchange of statements between the Supreme Court and the country's Attorney General is strange inasmuch as it establishes that we seem to operating in a no man's land as far as the justice dispensation system is concerned.

Before closing the chapter, let's once again look at the PIL filed by Prakash Singh, the Supreme Court's landmark Judgment of 2006 and the directions to the Central and State governments for speedy implementation of those directives. The Judgment had clearly stated that "the commitment, devotion and accountability of the police has to be only to the rule of law" and that "the supervision and control has to be such that it ensures the police serve the people without any regard, whatsoever, to the status and position of any person while investigating a crime or taking preventive measures." The Supreme Court issued clear directives to insulate the police from political or other extraneous pressures brought about on them. Autonomy and independence in this respect has been considered extremely important by all the commissions and committees appointed by the various governments. Justice K T Thomas, who was appointed by the Supreme Court in 2008 to monitor the implementation of its directions, expressed his dismay over the total indifference to the issue of police reforms by the states. Justice J S Verma, who submitted a comprehensive report on the amendments to the criminal law in 2012, urged the states to comply with all the directions issued by the Supreme Court but, according to him, the executive arm of the states was not willing to let go of the authority they currently enjoyed under the present system.

Two drafts for replacing the presently applicable Police

Act enacted by the British in 1861 are already available but, unfortunately, the successive Central governments have shown no interest in enacting the new law. There seems to be a subtle understanding reached between the Central and State governments at the cost of any concern for public interest. Seventeen states have, in the meantime, enacted their own laws to replace the British Act in their respective states. While the British had only one Police Act for the whole country, we will end up with every state having its own individual police laws. The very idea of having senior police officers from All India Service, which was meant to keep the country unified and uniformly governed, has been thrown out of the window.

Most senior police officers are of the opinion that there is no lack of intent or desire in the police force to exercise neutrality in discharging their duty. But, very high level of political interference does not allow them to act in a non-partisan manner. Political interference, threat of transfers, punishment, tarnishing of personal service records, etc. play havoc with the system. It is also true that some senior police officers themselves create unholy alliances with politicians. This has not stopped even after the Supreme Court directives. The root cause of the problem is 'we the people'. As long as we elect people who are not just undeserving but also undesirable, we will continue suffering this state of affairs. It is time we wake up and start casting our precious vote only for such candidates who have the abilities and the intent to bring about the required change. The apparent nexus between politicians, bureaucrats and the police has to be broken, and the only way this can be attempted is by making sure that the quality of people who are the primary drivers and responsible for this malaise, the elected representatives, is improved. It would take quite some time for the electorate to get educated and sensitised to a level at which they start believing that we deserve something better than what is on offer; that is the time the foundations of a healthy democracy will be laid.

Waiting For Justice Interminably

"All the rights secured to the citizens under the Constitution are worth nothing, and a mere bubble, except guaranteed to them by an independent and virtuous Judiciary."

—Andrew Jackson

(Seventh President of USA)

"There is no client as scary as an innocent man."

—J. Michael Haller

(Criminal Defense Attorney)

INDIAN DEMOCRACY stands on three pillars: 1. the Legislature; 2. the Executive; and 3. the Judiciary. While the executive and legislative are, to a large extent interwoven, Judiciary is supposed to stand alone and be absolutely independent. The Indian Constitution requires it to be so. Various governments have tried to subvert this independence of Judiciary but, fortunately, the institution has survived these onslaughts. We need to give a part of the credit to some of the strong personalities that have been a part of the Supreme Court bench. Strong public opinion against such attempts also worked decisively for governments to ultimately back off from their attempts.

The Indian judicial system has a long history and is one of the oldest legal systems in the world.[1] The system is based on both legislation and common law but, in the present scenario, convergence of both can easily be felt. Common law was developed in England primarily from judicial decisions based on customs and precedents, unwritten in statutes or code, and constituting the bases of English legal system. In India the judicial system is made effective through the Constitution of India. The system consists of three hierarchical layers of justice dispensation institutions—the Supreme Court, the High Courts, and the Subordinate Courts. Hierarchical structure of the judicial system is as under.[2]

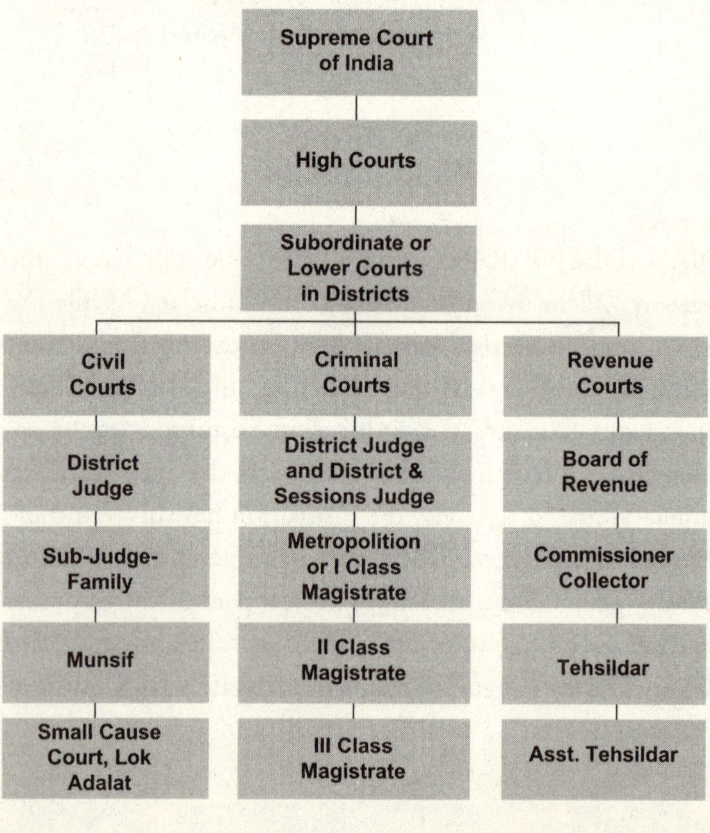

A strong legal system is the backbone of any civilization. The primary objective of a judicial system is to ensure the rule of law and legal security for citizens. The rule of law means that the administration of justice and the exercise of public authority must be predictable and consistent and must be conducted to high standards. The independence of judiciary, enshrined in our Constitution, is the cornerstone of our democratic society and a safeguard for the freedom and rights of our citizens under the rule of law. It means that judges should be free to pronounce judgments that are impartial and based solely on facts and legal provisions without interference, pressure or influence from the State or individual or a group of individuals. Social, economic and political justice is part of the Preamble of our Constitution. The guarantee of equality of law and equal protection of law lies at the heart of our judicial system. The right to life encapsulates the essence of all the rights and liberties—this has been universally acknowledged and repeatedly held by our Supreme Court. Timely justice and speedy trial is a facet of the right to life under our Constitution. Ensuring equal access to justice, a constitutional mandate not just in terms of a fundamental right but also a good governance directive under the Constitution, is fraught with multiple constraints. Our Supreme Court is supposed to place the citizens and their needs at the core of these concerns in ensuring access to justice.

SUPREME COURT

The President of India nominates judges to this Court. The Indian Constitution under Article 124(1) states that there shall be a Supreme Court of India consisting of the Chief Justice of India (CJI) and 7 judges. The number of judges, through the process of laws passed by the Parliament, has increased to 34 over the years. The role and position of the Supreme Court is vital in the judicial and political system of India. The Supreme Court is the highest court in India and has the ultimate judicial authority to interpret the Constitution and decide questions of national law (including local bylaws). The Supreme Court is also vested with the power of judicial review to ensure the application of the rule of law.

Inter alia, the Supreme Court of India has the following functions / jurisdictions:[3]

- Original Jurisdiction
- Appellate Jurisdiction
- Constitutional Appeal
- Civil Appeal
- Criminal Cases Appeal
- Special Appellate Jurisdiction
- Right to hear Appeal against decision of Special Court
- Protection of Constitution
- Power to interpret the Constitution
- Power of Judicial Review
- Court of Records
- Administrative Functions

The Supreme Court of India has a collegium which appoints judges to the constitutional court; the system has its genesis in three of its own judgments which are collectively known as Three Judges Case: 1. SP Gupta vs Union of India-1982, 2. Supreme Court Advocates-on-Record Association vs Union of India-1993, and 3. In Special Reference 1 of 1998, the Court evolved the principle of judicial independence to mean that no other branch of the State, including the legislature and executive, would have any say in the appointment of judges. A judge of the Supreme Court retires on attaining 65 years of age. The tenure of the judge is dependent upon his/her appointment from High Court or directly as the Supreme Court judge. Appointment of the CJI is based upon the seniority among the judges (though there have been exceptions) of the Supreme Court. The CJI also retires on attaining the age of 65 years. The Supreme Court has filled up the entire sanctioned strength of 34 judges.[4] The Court's lowest bench consists of two judges and is known as Division Bench. Then comes the Full Bench which consists of three or more judges but less than five. The last is known as the Constitutional Bench which has five or more (no upper limit on the numbers—there has been a 13 judge bench in the past). Unlike in other countries (in USA all the 12 judges of their Supreme Court sit as one bench), our Supreme Court has a number of benches in session concurrently. Despite this practice, we continue to have a very large number of pending cases in this court.

HIGH COURTS OF INDIA

The genesis of our High Courts is in the British Raj. By Indian High Court Act of 1861 the Supreme and Sadar Courts were amalgamated. The Indian High Court Act of 1861 authorised the Queen of England to issue letters to erect and establish the High Courts of Calcutta, Madras and Bombay. It is noteworthy that the Act itself did not establish High Courts in India. The objective of the Act was to amalgamate Supreme and Sadar Courts in the three presidencies of Calcutta, Bombay and

Madras. The jurisdiction, power and responsibilities of the two amalgamated courts were to be exercised by these three High Courts. Each High Court comprised of a Chief Justice and regular judges not exceeding 15. All judges could hold office at the pleasure of the British Crown. The High Court of Calcutta established on 14 May 1862 has the distinction of being the first High Court since it came into existence before the High Courts in Bombay and Madras were established on 26 June 1862. On 17 March 1866, the North West Provinces also got their own High Court at Agra. This Court was shifted to Allahabad in 1869. This is how the story of High Courts in India began.

Now we have High Courts at the state and union territory level of India, which together with the Supreme Court of India at the national level, comprise the country's judicial system. Each High Court has jurisdiction over a state, a union territory or a group of states and union territories. Below the High Courts in the hierarchy are the subordinate courts such as civil courts, family courts, criminal courts and various other district courts. High Courts are instituted as constitutional courts under Part 6, Chapter 5, Article 214 of the Indian Constitution. High Courts are principal courts of original jurisdiction in each state and union territory. However, High Courts exercise their original civil and criminal jurisdiction only if the subordinate courts are not authorised by the law to try such matters for lack of pecuniary and territorial jurisdiction. High Courts may also enjoy original jurisdiction in matters, if so designated, specifically in a state of federal law.

The work of most High Courts primarily consists of appeals on judgments from lower courts and writ petitions in terms of Article 226 of the Constitution. A writ petition is also an original jurisdiction of a High Court. The precise territorial jurisdiction of each High Court varies to an extent. The hierarchical appeal travels up from a tehsil kotwali to criminal/civil courts to district courts to High Court to Supreme Court. Each state is divided into judicial districts presided by a district and session judge. He/she is known as District Judge when presiding over a civil case and as a Sessions Judge when presiding over a criminal case. He is the highest judicial authority below a judge of the High Court. Below him, there are courts of civil jurisdiction known by different names in different states. Under Article 141 of the Constitution, all courts in India, including High Courts, are bound by the judgments and orders of the Supreme Court of India by precedence.

The judges of the High Courts are appointed by the President of India in consultation with the Chief Justice of India and the Governor of the respective state. A High Court is headed by a Chief Justice. The Chief Justice and judges of High Court rank fourteenth and seventeenth in the Indian order of precedence. The number of judges in a High Court is decided by dividing the average initiation of main cases during the last five years by the national average, or the average rate of disposal of main cases per judge per year in the High Court, whichever is higher. The Allahabad High Court is the largest court with a sanctioned strength of 160 judges (76 permanent and 84 additional judges) while Sikkim High Court is the smallest with only three permanent judges. Under the Constitution of India, every state should have one High Court. The Constitution of India has not made any detailed/clear description of the powers and functions of Indian High Courts unlike in the case of Supreme Court. The Constitution retains their functions to be same as these were before the promulgation of Indian Constitution, subject to the provisions of the Constitution and the laws made by the appropriate Legislature.

SUBORDINATE COURTS IN INDIA

Part VI, Chapter Vl of the Indian Constitution provides for subordinate courts as part of our judicial system. These courts are at the state level and are directly supervised by the respective State High Courts. Subordinate Courts are for every district or for one or more districts together, taking into account the number of cases and population distribution in the districts for administration of justice. The highest court in each district is that of District and Sessions Court. This is the principal court of original civil jurisdiction besides the High Court of the State which derives its jurisdiction in civil matters primarily from the Code of Civil Procedure. The District Court is also a Court of Sessions when it exercises its jurisdiction on criminal matters under the Code of Criminal Procedure. The District Court is presided over by a District Judge appointed by the governor of the state on the advice of the Chief Justice of the state. In addition to the district judge, there may be a number of additional district judges depending upon the work load. The judge and the court presided over by the additional district judge have equivalent jurisdiction as the District Judge and his District Court. The district judge, however, exercises supervisory control over additional and assistant district judges, including decisions on the allocation of work amongst them. Being the highest judge at the district level, the district judge also enjoys the powers to manage the state funds allocated for the development of judiciary in the district. The district judge is called 'Metropolitan Sessions Judge' when presiding over a District Court in a city which is designated a 'metropolitan area' by the state. Other courts that are subordinate to district court in the metropolitan area are, also, referred to with 'metropolitan' prefixed to the usual designation. An area is designated a metropolitan area by the state government if population of the area exceeds one million or more. There are 672 district courts in operation in the country.[5]

India has another set of courts instituted by Central Bureau of Investigation (CBI). This Bureau traces back its origins to the Special Police Establishment (SPE), a central police force which was set up in 1941 by then British Government to investigate bribery and corruption in transactions with the War and Supply Department of India. It had its headquarters in Lahore. After the end of the second world war, there was continued need for a central government agency to investigate bribery/corruption by central government employees. Sardar Patel, the first Deputy Prime Minister of independent India, who headed the Home Ministry as well, continued with this organisation. The establishment acquired the name of Central Bureau of Investigation (CBI) after independence.

The CBI Court is a trial court which registers cases for trials investigated by CBI for offenses punishable under Prevention of Corruption Act. It is really another sessions court established by the central government, in consultation with the Chief Justice of the respective High Court. Appeals against the order passed by the CBI court can be directly filed in the High Court of the relevant jurisdiction. The judges of the CBI court are appointed by the High Court and their normal tenure is 3 years on deputation. The number of cases dealt by CBI court is limited because of the high volume of evidences involved in each case.

VILLAGE COURTS

In order to reduce load on subordinate courts and to also bring delivery of justice to the doorsteps of the villagers, the Parliament of India enacted Gram Nyayalayas Act 2008 (village courts) for speedy and easy access to justice in widespread rural areas of India. The Act came into effect from 2 October 2009 (Mahatma Gandhi's Birth Anniversary). The Act, however, has not been enforced the way it was meant to be. As of now only 2,086 functional Gram Nyayalayas have been established in the country against a target of 5,000.[7] The reasons for such a poor show seem to be: a) financial constraints (finance is to be provided by the respective state governments); b) resistance of lawyers; and c) reluctance on the part of police and other state government officials. The fact is that state politicians and officials have shown no passion for the enactment of this very useful Act. Gram Nyayalayas are supposed to be established at the headquarters of every panchayat at intermediate level or a group of contiguous panchayats in a district where there is no panchayat at intermediate level. These Nyayalayas are to be presided over by a Nyayadhikari, who has the same power and enjoys the same salary and other benefits as that of a first class judicial magistrate.

Nyayadhkaris are to be appointed by the state governments in consultation with the High Court of the jurisdiction. Such Nyayalayas have jurisdiction over an area specified by a notification of the respective state government in consultation with respective High Court. Nyayalayas can also function as mobile courts within the notified jurisdiction and these function only after giving wide publicity of the same. These village courts have both civil and criminal jurisdiction over the offenses and nature of suits specified in the first, second and third schedule of the Act. The pecuniary jurisdiction of the Nyayalayas is fixed by the respective High Court. The fees charged for the civil suits shall not exceed Rs 100 irrespective of the value of property in dispute. Central as well as state governments can add or remove items from the schedule. While the central government can amend the list in schedule I and II by notifying them and, thereafter, tabling it in the Parliament, the State Government can amend the items in Part III of Schedule I or II, in the areas of law which the state government is competent to enact after due consultation with the respective High Court and notifying it. Such notification has to be laid in the State Legislature.

Criminal offenses in the Gram Nyayalayas are to be tried in a summary manner in accordance with chapter XXIA of Code of Criminal Procedure. The Act allows plea bargaining in accordance with chapter XXIA of criminal procedure. Appeals in criminal cases can be made to the sessions courts in the respective jurisdiction. These nyayalayas can follow special procedures in civil matters, in a manner they deem just and reasonable in the interest of justice. Civil suits must proceed on a day to day basis, with limited adjournments and are to be disposed of within a period of six months. Appeals on civil cases to the District Court have to be made within a period of one month from the date of the judgement. For execution of decree, the court may allow special procedures by following rules of natural justice. If possible, the nyayalayas should try for conciliation of dispute and the settlement in the early stages of trying the case. Nyayalayas have the powers to accept certain evidences which are otherwise not acceptable under the Indian Evidence Act.

We have a well-designed judicial system with an intend to deliver justice to all levels of society at an affordable cost. It is sufficiently elaborate and far reaching to make justice available at the doorsteps even to people living in remote corners of the country. The system has four levels starting at the bottom from village courts (Gram Nyayalayas) to the Supreme Court at the top. The Supreme Court, besides being the final court of appeal, is also the final authority on the interpretation and application of Indian Constitution. However well-designed and rolled out, the system has not produced the intended results particularly because of the inexhaustibly long time it takes to get justice. It has completely failed to cope with people's needs. The number of pending cases in different courts is astonishingly large and this only indicates the scale of failure of the justice dispensation system. If the judicial operating capabilities and the increase in the number of new cases and disposal per year remain at the same level, it is estimated that it will take more than 300 years to clear the backlog.[8] Ironically, despite this reality we all tend to believe that we in India have a robust judicial system. This backlog has obviously not accumulated overnight. The problem has been mounting over decades but has remained largely unattended.

CJI Justice Dipak Misra, not very long ago and while in office, had said that pendency should not be confused with arrears, and that more number of cases reflected faith in the judicial system. The objective, obviously, was to cover up a failure that has a huge impact on the loss of faith in judicial recourse.

He added that, "it is to be remembered that every delay is not an arrear. The concept of docket explosion is also a sign which signifies that the Indian citizenry reposes faith in the judicial system of the country and are approaching the courts in their quest for justice." According to Justice Misra, it is only those cases which are not disposed of within the stipulated period of time or within their case life that ultimately turn into an arrear. "Hence, we must not rush to declare every delay as an arrear and get into a state of disturbance by such ill-founded concepts." Leave alone being able to convince people by his arguments, he is seemingly skeptical about his position. At the same time, the CJI did admit that the problem of pendency and delays has to be accepted and the judiciary has been consciously investing in innovative strategies to tackle these issues. "Our concerted efforts to reduce and finally eliminate the five-year-old cases in the subordinate courts are befitting results. Arrears Committees of the High Courts have already been advised to supervise this issue and orchestrate a time-bound action plan to curtail the growth of such arrears," pointed out Justice Misra. Whatever actions may have been taken, the results are not visible—at least as of now.

He said that although in India there is a judge for approximately 19 million people, which is far lower as compared to other countries like USA and China, there has been focused approach to cut down arrears. Justice Misra referred to over 5,000[9] vacant posts in the subordinate judiciary, which is grappling with around 3 crore cases,[10] and said that the situation cannot be called satisfactory. "It is high time that we firmly resolve and prepare a pan-India action plan to eradicate the problem of vacancies in subordinate courts," emphasised the CJI, adding that the High Courts must act in coordination with the state governments concerned to improve the situation.

Justice Misra suggested that a review mechanism along with suitable guidelines on grouping of cases for prioritisation, timeline for disposal, alternative methods of dispute resolution, fast-tracking of certain cases etc. shall definitely help. "Explore options of Saturday Courts for cases other than criminal appeals. Every drop counts for it is commonplace that little drops of water make the mighty ocean. It is small things that add up to produce the huge. It is through persistent efforts and continued application that major accomplishments would finally result."

He sounded an alarm on the rising pendency at a time when the situation is almost getting out of hand with the backlog touching 33 million cases. While 27 million cases are pending in subordinate courts, the backlog clogging the High Courts is 4.3 lacs and in the Supreme Court it is around 60,000.[11] He showed a particular concern for the very large number of undertrials languishing in jails across the country without trials and bail. Of all the pending cases in the district and taluka courts, about 37 per cent are more than three years old while about 23 per cent are more than five years old.[12] In the Allahabad High Court, there are about 7.4 lac cases pending; out of these more than 40,000 are pending for more than 30 years.[13] There are more than 3.6 lac cases pending in district/ subordinate courts for a period between 20 to 30 years.[14]

These numbers are mind-boggling. Over 1,000 cases are in the process of being heard or being argued for the past 50 years or so.[15] Many cases are in a state of perpetual stay while others are simply given a new date of hearing but never taken up for final disposal without even recording of reasons. A case, for example, filed on 2 July 1953 by one Bhagwan against Dulari in Varanasi shows that the first hearing was held on 11 October 2015 (62 years later) without conclusion. Next hearing was posted on 15 July 2019. Would anyone in his right mind say or believe that our justice system is working—obviously not? It is a common belief that our courts take generations to settle civil cases by when the value of the property in dispute is completely lost or has dramatically changed. In cases of civil disputes, a lot of people (in a lot of cases) resort to other means, unethical at times, for settling their disputes promptly. As a matter of fact, there are gangs of goons operating in cities as well as in rural areas that specialise and thrive on this activity. It can easily be assumed that while people do have faith in the Indian judicial system, there is enough evidence emerging of people losing faith and resorting to resolving their problems through means that are unethical and illegal, at times criminal.

In 2014, former CJI RM Lodha, proposed to make Indian judiciary work through the year (his proposal was to skip the long vacations) to reduce the pendency of cases. This was proposed to be done without increase in working hours or the days of the individual judges and without their sacrificing their number of days for vacations. It only meant that different judges would be going on vacations in different periods of the year as per their choice. The Bar Council of India turned the proposal down because it would inconvenience the advocates who would have to work throughout the year. The excuse for turning down such a good proposal is indeed frivolous since the advocates could also have adopted similar way of working as suggested for judges. Obviously convenience of the advocates is more important than that of the public.

While Chief Justice Dipak Misra was able to diagnose the problem and speak candidly about it, he did not articulate any suggestions to improve the situation. According to him the situation was already alarming and seemed to be getting out of hand. It was expected that the CJI, who is the administrative chief of the entire Indian Judiciary, would have done something challenging and innovative while in office. No particular CJI can be held responsible for inaction as all of them have done the same thing—talked about the issues and discussed the problems in public but done precious little—in fact, nothing to overcome the mounting problem of delays in the system.

The figures on pendency of cases show a steep increase since 2012 and yet the Supreme Court does not seem to have taken any tangible steps to control the rate of growth. Most reports on the subject appear to have come to the conclusion that increase in the strength of judges along with improved infrastructure are necessary to improve the situation, and yet, very little seems to have been initiated. According to a report of Supreme Court of India titled *Subordinate Judiciary—Access to Justice 2016*, capacity constraints are the main reasons for high level of pendency. The report states that the mounting pendency of cases in subordinate courts is because the subordinate judiciary works under a severe shortage of courtrooms, secretarial and support staff and residential accommodation for judges. According to the report, the subordinate judiciary has been working with a deficiency of 5,018 courtrooms because existing 15,540 court halls are insufficient to cater to the strength of 20,558 judicial officers as on 31 December 2015, in addition to the shortfall of 41,775 staff positions. While that may be so, the inefficiency of the court proceedings is also deplorable. Gross inefficiency in dealing with the cases is surprisingly never talked about in most reports. This is because accepting inefficiency would require addressing the problem through internal process improvements while the problem of insufficient judges and courtrooms can be easily passed on to the government's inability to provide resources.

According to a report published by Dushyant Mahadik of Administrative Staff College of India (who seems have done a lot of good work on the subject), most cases listed on daily cause list do not get a hearing on any given date. A cursory look at the case status and history of case hearings shows a high percentage of court time being wasted due to absenteeism or lack of preparedness on the part of involved parties. Studies of a sample of cases with the help of *roznama* (register of cases) show meaningful court business was conducted only for 21 per cent of the cases on the given date. In other words, if a case is listed for hearing, there is only one in five chance that the case proceedings will actually take place on the given date. Court time is not utilised productively since four out of five cases are adjourned for proceedings for another date. People, who have had the experience of attending a subordinate court, recount their experience as tormenting. The other thing that most have expressed is that the absence of the accused is treated differently compared to the absence of the prosecutor. If the accused is absent on the given date, the possibility of a non-bailable warrant being issued against him is very high, whereas there is very little sternness shown in the event of the prosecutor being absent. In doing so, the judges have, at the subconscious level, already pronounced the accused as guilty. Possibility of getting the case heard being only about 20 per cent, the accused is expected to run to the court on every date that the court requires him. Adjournments are given on the flimsiest of grounds. In a recent personal experience, three adjournments were granted because the judge took unscheduled leave on the date of the hearing—once because he had to go out of station on some work and twice the prosecutor failed to appear on the date. These postponements accounted for the delay in the final hearing by over two years. The case was so flimsy that it was disposed of in less than an hour once the hearing started.

This is not surprising because it seems to be the norm. People associated with court work professionally and justice seekers have got used to this malaise. There is a strong case to streamline and systematise the working of subordinate courts as well as the High Courts to improve their efficiency. Shouldn't the prosecutors also be held responsible just as the defendants are when causing delays in hearing? There is a strong justification for carrying out extensive sensitisation and training programmes for judges in the subordinate judiciary to look at both the petitioners and defendants, as well as the accused and the prosecutor, as people who are fighting for what they think is their legal right and not be biased against one party, let alone putting that on display. The conduct of the advocates is also equally deplorable as they have a vested interest in seeking adjournments rather than arguing the case. More hearings not only mean more money but also deferment of professional preparedness to argue the matter. If only adjournments, which are generally given on rather flimsy pretexts are stopped, the courts could probably dispose of double the number of cases that they do now.

According to the report *Prison Statistics–2015* compiled by the National Crime Records Bureau, the number of undertrials at the end of 2015 was 2,82,076. Undertrials represented 67 per cent of the total inmates in prison. They are in jail because they are suspected to have committed a crime. Police have not found the time to complete the investigation of the suspected crime and, therefore, the undertrials must remain in jail. Police have not found time because our police force is politicised and, therefore, prefers to investigate only such cases that are politically sensitive or those in which politicians have some interest. Investigations are done only to meet the predetermined objective of proving them guilty or not guilty as required by the political bosses in power. There is no dearth of cases that can be cited to demonstrate the point. Almost 62 per cent of the undertrials are either illiterate or have not studied up to Class 10.[16] The breakup of the undertrials shows that 18.8 per cent are Muslims, 20.7 per cent belong to the scheduled castes and 11.5 per cent are tribals.[17] These numbers clearly indicate the huge problem that the country is faced with in respect of the prejudices that we carry regarding religion and castes. People who are languishing in jail are poor and belong to a religion or a caste that the ruling class has used for its political advantage but never made attempts to get them into the social or economic mainstream.

Some of them have remained in jail exceeding the punishment that could have been awarded to them for the suspected crime that they have supposedly committed, if they had been pronounced guilty of those crimes. If a person has remained in jail for over six months, has not been chargesheeted for any crime and is poor and not able to provide the bond, should he not be let free on giving his personal bond particularly when his Aadhar card number is available? A number of senior judges have made laudable statements about undertrials but have done nothing concrete to mitigate their sufferings. There are also some undertrials who do not wish to be released from jail because jail provides them with food and shelter—such is the scale of poverty in the country. They will starve once outside because there is hardly any chance of their getting jobs. And, even if they were to get a job, they would live with the discrimination and bigotry that they would be subjected to as part of polarised and desensitised society. Should we not have a scheme to provide jobs for a certain period to those who get released from jails?

Our Supreme Court today does not enjoy the exalted position that it once did. This has happened because of its own failures and doings. No one else can be blamed for such erosion of its credibility. The function of our Supreme Court is more than just to dispense justice on the cases brought to it. It is also to administer the entire justice dispensation system of the country. It is their duty to monitor the performance of the whole system and to take timely corrective action as and when necessary. People are not interested in the speeches of the outgoing Chief Justices about the alarming situation of the pending cases in the various courts. Nor are they interested in knowing the reasons for such an alarming situation. They are interested in knowing the concrete actions they have taken during their own tenure towards mitigating the mounting problems. What concrete steps have they really taken to stop piling up of unattended cases to such a level that the public has started having doubts about the competence of the judiciary and the judicial system as such? It is strange that the Chief Justices should talk on this subject when retiring as if someone else is to be blamed for the situation that is created. The apex court must admit that it is actually denying justice to millions of countrymen by the inordinate delays. It is meaningless to award justice to the aggrieved when he is dead and gone. And this is happening quite frequently, if not as a routine. The fact is that our top court is not aware of what is happening in the subordinate courts. The problem really is not a shortage of judges or the infrastructure as is routinely believed and claimed. The problem is one of routine adjournments of cases in subordinate courts for the flimsiest of reasons. Unless the subordinate courts improve their efficiency in disposal of cases, increase in the number of cases will keep compounding. Is it not sufficient to allow one chance each to both the litigants for their failure to appear? Also, the court should hear the cases in one go without adjournments. We need to have clear and strict norms for allowing adjournments; these should be an exception and not a rule. With such improved practices, the courts will dispose of the cases three times faster and at the same time reduce the harassment that the aggrieved parties have to go through routinely. If we have to modify the age-old Indian Evidence Act of 1872 (a 150 year old act promulgated by the British) for this purpose, so be it. We could also use video recording to process the case faster.

Not very long ago, four seniormost judges of the Supreme

Court aired their grievances in the open (at a press conference) against the Chief Justice of India on the method of assigning judges to the various benches. Though not mentioned specifically, they were clearly airing their suspicion that the Chief Justice of India was assigning judges to influence the final judgement. They felt that assignment of judges on the benches should be done in consultation with the senior judges in a transparent manner. The correct method for CJI would have been to adopt the age-old democratic method of sitting together and developing a consensus on the contentious issue raised by the four senior judges. It so happened that there was also a public interest litigation (PIL) pending in court on the very subject of assignment of judges to the benches. The method, the litigants felt, was arbitrary and lacked transparency. If the CJI had changed his method and agreed to consensus between the judges, the litigants would have had no case to pursue. Unfortunately, the CJI stirred the matter further by nominating himself to the bench to hear the PIL in a case in which he was an interested party and, as expected, the bench gave the verdict in favour of CJI, clearing the way for nomination of judges on the bench as his sole responsibility.

Surprisingly, the four judges who had almost revolted against him did nothing further in the matter. Obviously, they either developed cold feet or had differences among themselves. Nothing further was heard in the matter. The whole episode was shameful and did not yield anything. One of the four became the CJI and one wonders if, after becoming CJI, he has changed the method of nominating judges to various benches. No doubt we have a very large number of judges in the Supreme Court and there are bound to be differences amongst them but one would expect that the institution responsible for protection of country's democracy be run democratically and in an exemplary manner. The public perception is that it was a serious lapse on the part of the then CJI to chair a bench in a case in which he was an interested party. Also, the four judges who had perceptibly revolted should have continued with what they had set out to achieve. These two episodes have, unfortunately, brought down the stature of the Supreme Court further by quite a few notches.

There is a growing public perception of increasing irrelevance of Supreme Court primarily because of the fact that their verdicts directing the government are not taken seriously. This is a very dangerous development. If the judgments of the Supreme Court are ignored and not implemented even in letter, leave alone in spirit, people are bound to feel that our highest court has become toothless and has no powers to ensure that their judgments/directions are implemented. Take the case of the PIL of Prakash Singh (retd police chief of UP) vs the Union of India, filed in the Supreme Court in 1996. He petitioned the Supreme Court under Article 321B, for the issue of directions to the Government of India to frame a new Police Act on the lines of the model Act drafted by the National Police Commission established in 1977 in order to ensure that the police is made accountable primarily to the law of the land and the people of the country. (This case has been discussed in detail in the earlier chapter). In a historic verdict delivered on 22 September 2006, the Supreme Court issued 7 directives to the Central and State Governments for immediate implementation.

The underlying objective was to make the working of

police force independent from interference by the politicians and by bureaucrats. It is 14 years now since the directives were issued but the hold on the police force by the politicians and bureaucrats has only increased. The Supreme Court, also, has not shown any interest in demanding implementation of its directives even though it is well known that political interference is plaguing the police force. The lack of fear for not implementing a Supreme Court directive is very visible in this case. One does not have to point out specific instances (there are numerous) where one sees that police has acted either wrongly or with a strong bias in favour of politicians and bureaucrats. One sees biased police action(s) almost every day. Victims that are involved are invariably poor and from lower castes or from minority groups. It would not be out of place for the citizens of the country to believe that the Supreme Court is a little hesitant to take a stand against the government.

Let us look at another case where the direction of the apex Court was ignored. Against a PIL filed on inhuman conditions in prisons across the country, an order passed by a three-judge bench led by CJI Justice RM Lodha on 5 September 2014 ordered that the government release thousands of undertrials languishing in various jails across the country. Justice Lodha said the Judiciary was witness to men and women detained in prison for years, sometimes for more time than they would have spent had they been found guilty. He also observed that undertrials who are entitled to bail have not been able to get it because they are very poor and have nobody to help them provide the required bail bond. While issuing the said order the court simultaneously mobilised judicial officers across the country to visit every prison in their respective districts in the next two months to identify and release undertrial prisoners who had already undergone detention for half the maximum period of imprisonment for their alleged offence prescribed under the law. The court, however, clarified that the release did not apply for undertrials whose offence attracts death penalty. One has no doubt that the judicial officers so mobilised would have identified such prisoners, as instructed by the CJI, for the government authorities to take the matter forward to effect the release of such identified prisoners. But, unfortunately, that did not happen. A Division Bench consisting of Justice Madan and Justice Deepak Gupta expressed concern on 10 October 2017 as to why the undertrials were not released by the states (despite the apex court's direction given three years earlier) even after completion of their full sentences. Clearly the order passed by CJI Justice Lodha went unheeded and was ignored by the government authorities. Such is the respect our elected governments have for the directives issued by our Apex Court.

Relevance of our Supreme Court is a very important issue for our democracy. Who is supposed to correct this situation is a question that needs to bother every educated citizen? If the perception that the Supreme Court orders are not executed by the State is created, the fear of losing respect for the judicial system of the country becomes pronounced; this will have a colossal detrimental impact on the functioning of our democracy and will also impact the law and order situation in the country.

One would think that the burden of restoring the powers and the status of the Supreme Court lies with the President of the country since all the three arms of governance—the legislature, the executive and the judiciary are his responsibility. Under the present circumstances the restoration of our Supreme Court's stature is not likely to happen in the foreseeable future which is unfortunate. We abandoned the true principles of democracy a long time ago when we started electing presidents that were politically affiliated and not guardians of the Constitution. The constitutional head of a hugely diverse country like India has to be an eminent intellectual and not a politician. Why did the Constituent Assembly decide for an indirect election of the President of the country as against a direct franchise is something that needs to be looked at? Politicians affiliated to a particular political party should not be the constitutional head of the country. Every government would, invariably, want the President to toe the line they (the government) dictate and act as a rubber stamp. We, as a result, have had presidents who were strongly aligned to government (read political party) and not to the Constitution of India. This practice of electing presidents on the basis of allegiance started decades ago, in 1969 to be precise. If this practice had not started, we would not have had Emergency imposed in our country in 1975. Maybe a direct election is the answer, and this is possible by way of a major change in the Constitution.

We also need revamping of all our vital democratic institutions to bring back faith in the working of our democracy. Nehru's vision of democracy was not what we have ended up with in the last seven decades.

It is disturbing to see our Supreme Court becoming an institution involved in high-value litigation with little time to worry about the failing judicial delivery system in the lower courts. It needs to acknowledge its failure and must take urgent actions to do whatever is necessary to get the system back on rails. Our belief that we, in India, have a good and working judicial system is fast eroding. It does appear that our Supreme Court finds comfort in maintaining status quo in the well-entrenched traditions of the British who left India long time ago. Take for example, CJI Lodha's proposal for courts to work through the year without going on annual vacation. This, it seems, was shot down by the advocates' lobby. Most factories in India work round the clock, seven days a week and in some cases even on festival days to produce wealth for the nation. Everyone in our country works for 48 hours a week in comparison to the western countries that work 40 hours a week. France, in fact, has only 36 work hours in a week. India is a poor country and, therefore, people have to put in extra hours of work to catch up with the West.

Why should our courts be an exception? Why should the courts not work round the year, six days a week, particularly since they have a huge backlog to clear which is causing a lot of hardship to people at large? No one is stopping the judges and their support staff from availing their due vacations every year as is done by other professionals. In the extraordinary situation that exists today, the authorities should even consider the subordinate courts working two shifts a day to overcome infrastructural constraints. The primary job of courts is to deliver justice and do that on time. Whatever is necessary to be done to achieve that should be done. We follow English Law but that does not bind us to follow their practices and traditions of working hours. Every country has its own problems and it is our duty to evolve and change according to the need of the hour. CJIs are appointed, serve their term and move on and the serious problem of pending cases only gets talked about but never gets addressed.

Our judicial system needs major reforms and these are needed immediately. The last CJI was one of the four Supreme Court judges who brought their grievances into public domain. It was expected that on assuming office he would set the process of reforming the justice system in motion. *The Indian Express* dated Tuesday, 16 July 2019 reported that nine months after the Supreme Court's in-house think tank, Centre for Research and Planning, which was set up with an ambitious mandate to reform the judiciary seemed to be virtually disbanded. Handpicked by CJI Justice Ranjan Gogoi to head the CRP, Professor Mohan Gopal quit in March 2019 without citing any reasons, and no move for any fresh appointment to the Centre has been made since his exit. CRP was CJI Gogoi's brainchild and setting it up was one of the first decisions he took after assuming office in October 2018. It was intended to improve public confidence in the judiciary.

There have been a lot of unjust punishments meted out which are a serious blot on the functioning of our judicial system. While all cases of miscarriage of justice are not only due to judiciary, the fact remains that our judicial system has aggravated the suffering of the victims of miscarriage of justice. No doubt instances of miscarriage of justice have been reported by many countries but the number of such cases is far too small in civilized countries compared to our country.

Take the case of Nambi Narayanan working for the Indian Space Research Organisation (ISRO) on a very important assignment of developing cryogenic rocket engine. He was wrongly implicated in 1994, along with a few others, for supposedly leaking technical details of the project. He was released on bail after spending 50 days in jail. The problem is that it took over four long years to clear him of the charges.[18] No one has been questioned about the reasons for taking four years to process the case. His career, which was very promising and enviable, was marred for no reason. This, indeed, is a shame on our justice system.

In another case, Dr Narayan Waman Nerurkar was working for the Department of Electronics. In 1987, Nerurkar was accused of leaking test reports of a radar manufactured by a well-known German firm, which had been offered to the Indian army. Strangely enough, the packet containing the copies of the reports was opened by the courier company (which is not normal). In another strange coincidence the CBI officer happened to be in the office of the courier company at the time when the packet was opened. Another packet yielded the specifications of a helicopter required by our army. On the basis of the contents found in the two packets, the CBI instituted a case implicating Nerurkar and four others under Official Secrets Act, etc. While the trials were in progress, CBI withdrew cases against one of the accused. The cases against the other four went on for three long decades. Two of the accused died during this period. In their final verdict, the CBI acquitted all the four saying that there was no proof that either the test report of the radar or the specification of the helicopter constituted a secret document under the preview of Official Secrets Act. And, also, that there was no proof that the four accused knew each other, leave alone conspired to leak the documents.[19] Imagine the enormity of injustice meted out to the four individuals. They suffered the shame for three decades for no fault of theirs. Should some people not be punished for: a) initiating such a case; and b) taking three decades to come to the inevitable conclusion? The courts should have taken full blame for the delay in concluding the case and the people responsible for such enormous injustice should have been punished. Nothing of that sort happened.

The Indian Express of 26 July 2019 had a story captioned "We are acquitted but who will bring back (23) years". The case dates back to 22 May 1996 when a bomb blast in a bus near Samleti village in Duasa, on the Jaipur-Agra highway, killed 14 people and injured 37 others. The bus was headed to Bikaner from Agra. The blast came the day after the Lajpat Nagar bomb blast in Delhi in which 13 people were killed. The chargesheet named Ahmed Baja (42), Ali Bhatt (48), Mirza Nisar (39), Abdul Goni (57), and Rayees Beg (56). According to the chargesheet, they had conspired with Abdul Hameed, the main accused. They were released after spending 23 long years in jail on 23 July 2019. While acquitting them, the High Court observed that the prosecution had failed to provide evidence of conspiracy. It said the prosecution could not establish any link between them and the main accused, Abdul Hameed, whose death sentence was upheld. The life of these five individuals, who spent 23 years in jail, was totally ruined. What must they be feeling and how are their families expected to react is anybody guess? If those who have spent 23 years in jail, and their family members developed disdain for our judicial system, and the country as a whole, would it not be justified? There are many such cases which can be cited. We have to account for scores of lives ruined for no fault of theirs. Police personnel responsible for charging people with unjustified, non-bailable criminal offences leading to unjust confinements should also be considered as criminals and held responsible for their acts. People at the bottom rung of our societies are a convenient target for the police force to assign criminality to show quick results in solving criminal cases. This is done in connivance with the lower judiciary. These are common occurrences in our country.

The difference between a civilized nation and an anarchist nation lies in the way the nation upholds and enforces constitutional rights of all its citizens. Efficient working of the judicial system becomes fundamental to civilization and democracy. The system has to be efficient to be able to deliver justice on time and to punish only the guilty. It becomes mandatory that cases of those suspected to have committed crimes are dealt with expeditiously and those not found guilty are set free with their social standing unscathed and intact. On this scale, our judicial system is not only performing very poorly but failing completely. It is time we corrected this before it is too late.

The Supreme Court of India holds responsibility for delivering justice to the aggrieved in time and at the least cost. The public has the right to judge their performance in respect of these two parameters. We all know that they are running decades behind schedule on the timeline. Cost to the litigant is directly proportional to the time the litigant spends in fighting the case. The cost the litigant incurs is in paying advocates based on the number of appearances they make; most advocates can be quite expensive. In fact, some of them are prohibitively expensive. This is besides the time wasted in running up and down to the court whenever required to appear in person. Cost of delay and anxiety punishes the litigants very hard. Anyone who has had experience would know how frustrating the process can be. There is no realisation of the suffering that such delays cause to the litigants. Supreme Court judges sit in comfortable offices not willing to give up old British traditions of having long vacations while the pending cases continue to pile up. High Courts and other subordinate courts follow their lead and have similar work schedules oblivious of the suffering of people seeking justice.

Whatever reforms necessary in the system must be undertaken immediately without any further delay. Correction to the system involves: a) those related to Supreme Court alone; b) those that involve Supreme Court and executive branch of government; and c) those that involve Supreme Court, executive (including police) and the legislature. Let us first focus on those reforms which can be implemented by Supreme Court on its own. Many suggestions have been made by various NGOs and individuals on desirable reforms. Important issues that need to be resolved are: a) simplification of the process of dealing with cases which presently is extremely non-productive and tortuous; b) shortage of judges; c) shortages of infrastructure; and d) reforms in the functioning of Supreme Court itself. As pointed out earlier, while all those whose cases are listed are obliged to be present, an average of only 20 per cent of the listed cases are really dealt with on the given date. The rest are rescheduled to different dates. About 80 per cent of the people who make themselves present in the courts have to go back to reappear on the rescheduled date. A wasted day means loss of earnings and, in addition, the cost of appearing in court, which in some cases is considerable if travelling from far off places. Proper planning and timely listing and hearing of cases are very important in delivering justice. Ideally, there should be fast listing of cases with limited adjournments. Request for adjournments arises because either party is not ready with the case or when they cannot appear on the appointed day. Similar yardstick is to be applied to both the parties, even if one of the parties is the State. If the judge on the bench is convinced about the validity of the reasons forwarded by either party, he may allow adjournment but only once and no more. This will ensure that all the listed cases, by and large, will be heard on the given date.

Another important change in the working of the judicial process, which has been recommended by many including the Law Commission of India, is that the cases should be heard continuously and adjournments avoided once the hearing commences. This will ensure speedy verdict. These two suggestions, if implemented, will go a long way in delivering justice on time and without harassment to the people involved. Ideally, people involved in the case should be called to appear in the court only once (perhaps twice) for disposal of their case and no more. The corridors of courts in India—Subordinate and High Courts are like fish markets with no place to stand or sit. The basic infrastructure in courts such as toilets and canteen are unable to cope with the numbers wanting to use these facilities. It is time we make the appearance of the courts more litigant friendly. Speedy disposal will reduce the need for additional infrastructure. Steps suggested above will also speed up the cases and will help in clearing the backlog of cases in courts. Efficient disposal of cases is the only way to deliver justice.

While there is a continuous clamour for more judges and infrastructure, the number of days the courts work presently in a year is an eye opener. The Supreme Court works for 193 days in a year, High Courts work for 210 days and trial courts for 245 days.[20] In the case of Supreme Court, of the 13 Courts, one court is always in session and available seven days a week and on holidays to deal with cases which are urgent and cannot wait. Taking that into consideration, Judges of the Supreme Court work for 225 days in a year; this leaves 140 non-working days for them every year. Similarly, there is a colossal waste of time of the judges of the subordinate and high courts. Their infrastructure remains unutilised in this period of no work. While the courts may be justified in asking for more judges they must show full utilisation of what they have.

Providing infrastructure for Subordinate Courts and High Courts lies with the respective states. Since most states do not have the resources, people will continue to suffer till resources are made available. Lack of adequate resources is, indeed, the situation with every sector (not just the Judiciary) in our country. We must consider working of these courts (subordinate and high courts) round the year, all seven days a week, to provide 30 per cent extra working days to help clear the backlog and to cope with the incoming new cases. This will solve the problem of inadequacy of infrastructure to a great extent. This will, of course, require extra judges.

With regard to shortage of judges, almost all legal bodies and experts have unanimously recommended having a separate judicial service cadre to create a large pool of trained and dedicated judges. This will help get over the perennial problem of shortage of judges. This will also help in streamlining the problem of elevation of judges to fill vacancies that arise at higher levels without wasting time, as and when the need arises. There is a very strong case for accepting this recommendation considering the large number of judges required in India to run the system efficiently. At the end of 2017, we had a sanctioned strength of 22,704 judges to man subordinate courts and 1,079 judges for High Courts.[21] Considering that the working life of judges is around 35 years, about 3 per cent of the total strength i.e., around 717 judges should be retiring every year. There will be further attrition of around 500 judges per year for various other reasons. With time we will also have need for additional judges to cope with increasing flow of cases in the courts. This sort of requirement can only be met by having a separate academy for recruitment and training to replace the yearly attrition plus additional requirement of judges.

While a lot of thought is required to create this new organisation, it is felt that it should be similar to what we have for our army i.e., we should recruit legal graduates and train them in a dedicated academy and indoctrinate them to serve the justice dispensation system of the nation diligently and honestly. Promotions, in service life, should be on the basis of seniority alone but with two strong and meaningful filters—one before promotion to becoming a High Court judge and another before elevation to the Supreme Court. Those reaching a certain age, if not found suitable for elevation to higher courts, should be retired just as in the case of Indian army. Retirement of such people is very necessary to retain quality, keep upgrading judges in position and keep up the morale at all times. This additional attrition will mean additional annual recruitment at the entry level. This, if implemented, should go a long way in solving the problem of manning the justice system efficiently.

As far as reforms which involve Judiciary as well as executive (including police) are concerned, we have to really look for two reforms: 1. Depoliticising of police force; and 2. Creating an independent monitoring body with members of the Judiciary, Law Commission, and the Bar Council of India to ensure the judgments and directives issued by courts are implemented in letter and spirit.

The question that arises is whether Central Government is responsible for the implementation of the directives/verdicts of the Supreme Court or if the States are directly responsible to the Court for implementation of the same? It is necessary to define and separate responsibilities of the Central and State Governments in respect of the court's verdicts/directives. This will go a long way to make people believe and have faith in the country's judicial process and system.

No one can deny the veracity of the Gram Nyayalayas Act 2008 that came into force from 2 October 2009. Non-implementation of this very important and potentially effective Act is the sad part of the story. With the current rate of implementation it will perhaps take another 50 years for the Act to become effective across the country. General apathy of the authorities in our country towards the people and their issues is our biggest problem. While the initial expenditure for establishing these courts is to be provided by the Central Government, the implementation of the Act is the responsibility of the State Governments. According to the latest available report, only 208 courts are actually in operation. Since the country's judicial system has a lot at stake in this endeavour, the state governments need to establish these village courts without any further delay. This will help improve the efficiency of the judicial system considerably.

A lot needs to be done by the most revered institution—the

Supreme Court. For an ordinary man, seeking justice from the Supreme Court can be a nightmare. Some recent judgments and the delay in taking up some other cases have caused a lot of unrest in the minds of people. Trust deficit vis-a-vis the apex court has increased manifold. It can only be hoped that someday someone will ensure that the tenets of the Constitution of India are upheld. Only the rich or really desperate can knock on the doors of the Supreme Court. Advocates and solicitors charge unbelievably high fees for preparing cases and for appearing in Court; the primary reason for that is that they are continuously leveraging the perception of advocates' capabilities and the reputation that they have created for themselves with the bar and the bench. The stakes for litigants who reach the Supreme Court are so high that they do not mind getting into debt traps to afford the legal expenses. It is the duty of the Supreme Court to apply brakes to the monopolistic practice followed by this select set of advocates and solicitors. There should be some economic rationale to the fees that are charged. Even if most of the cases are fought by the corporate houses defending themselves against the government or other corporate houses, it does not mean that advocates should charge exorbitant fees. Individuals, obviously, cannot afford such costs. There has to be some regulation to ensure that the justice system remains within the reach of the common man. It defies logic that in a country where the head of the state is on a salary of Rs 5 lacs a month, an A league advocate should be charging Rs 25 lacs for a court appearance.

There are a few other issues that require addressing and are causing a lot of disquiet in the minds of the public: a) Election Commission; b) Increasing criminalisation of politics.

A standard argument given is that the accused cannot be held guilty unless proved beyond doubt. That of course is true insofar as punishment to the guilty is concerned for the alleged crime. This argument should not cover the candidature of an accused for election to the legislature. For the purpose of eligibility for contesting an election, the public must have candidates who have a blemish-free record. Chargesheeted candidates cannot be considered as having blemish-free record. Many petitions to stop criminalisation of politics have been dealt by various benches of the Supreme Court but have not been able to stop the increasing trend of this phenomenon. The trend of criminals in public office continues to increase at an alarming rate. The increasing trend indicates that criminals could be the majority in the Lok Sabha in not too distant a future.

Of the 519 MPs elected to the Lok Sabha in 2009, 86 had criminal records. In the 2019 elections, the number increased to 233 out of the total elected 539 members. The number of people with criminal records who are expected to legislate for the country has increased 2.7 times in the last two elections. If the trend continues, it would not be surprising that the entire population of legislators would be people with some criminal record and they, between themselves, would perhaps legislate that having a proven criminal record is a precondition for contesting Lok Sabha elections.

While innumerable cases have been filed in the Supreme Court, it has time and again stated that our Constitution does not have provisions to disqualify chargesheeted candidates from contesting elections under the Representation of People (RP) Act. Candidates are barred from running for office only after being convicted in criminal cases. Niranjan Sahoo and Bhawna

Agarwal in their article *Crime-political nexus: Can courts alone break it?* reported on the latest judgement pronounced on 25 September 2018 by the five-judge Constitution Bench headed by the then CJI Justice Dipak Misra. The bench declined to bar candidates with chargesheets in criminal cases from running for public office but issued directives to Election Commission to curb criminalisation of politics. Highlighting the importance of full disclosure to public, this important judgement gave its five directives: a) candidates must fill in the prescribed form; b) candidate must fill in bold letters that he is implicated in some crime; c) candidates must inform their party that they are implicated in some crime; d) on receiving information from candidates about their criminal antecedents, the party must put this information on its website; and e) the criminal antecedents should be published by the candidates and their party in newspapers which are widely circulated in the locality.

In short, the 100 page judgement by the Supreme Court explicitly cited concern over the sufferance of Indian democracy because of the increasing trend of criminalisation of politics. The key takeaway of the judgement was the Court urging the legislative branch to frame a 'strong' law that would make it obligatory for political parties to remove leaders charged with "heinous and grievous" crimes such as murder, rape and kidnapping and deny tickets to the offenders. As expected, all the political parties in India were opposed to the implementation of the five directives awarded in the judgement. Not only that, the judgement was not implemented and is not likely to be implemented in the foreseeable future. Yet another case when Supreme Court directives have been ignored.

Criminalisation of politics is not new in India. Way back

in 1993, NN Vohra (then Home Secretary, GOI) Committee documented the nexus between criminals, politicians and bureaucrats but this explosive report was never made public. This nexus has been flourishing for a long time primarily because criminals have become an important source of illegal funding for political parties in elections. Criminals provide lots of money to the political parties in return for getting tickets to contest elections. This is precisely the reason for increasing presence of criminals in our legislature. The Judiciary and Election Commission have already thrown up their hands in helplessness and despair. Politicians are in a position to decriminalise public offices but are vehemently opposed to such a move. Their interest is getting more funds to contest elections and not in cleaning up the system. This shows the level of concern our politicians have for preserving and nurturing a healthy democracy. We have brought this catastrophe on ourselves by continuing to elect totally undesirable and unworthy candidates as our legislators. The blame squarely rests with all of us.

Legislators having criminal records have been involved in murders, rape, kidnapping, abduction, etc. There are even cases of victims being punished instead of the alleged criminal because these criminals turned politicians enjoy covert protection from their political party in power and the police is more than a willing partner in the process. The actual situation on the ground has deteriorated to such an extent that even lodging of an FIR by the victim (or victim's relative) has become impossible or hazardous unless public pressure is brought upon the officers concerned. In a recent case, when the father of the rape victim went to the police station to complain and to lodge an FIR, he (not the alleged criminal) was taken into custody and beaten up mercilessly. He died a few days later as a result of the torture. The criminal in this case happened to be a powerful wealthy ex-legislator. Criminality in politics has already become far too powerful a force than what is generally perceived by people. We must vote only for candidates who have a proven and unblemished record of serving people; who are honest, trustworthy and capable and have genuine concern for the people and the country. The famous, celebrated third President of United States, Thomas Jefferson, who is credited with authoring the Declaration of Independence of United States said, "The spirit of resistance to the government is so valuable on certain occasions, that I wish it is always kept alive".

Diminishing Democracy

In a democracy the poor will have more power than the rich, because there are more of them, and the will of the majority is supreme.

Aristotle
(Greek Philosopher)

Governments without the separation of power commit the worst crimes.

James Cook
(British Explorer)

FOR SEVEN decades people in India and around the world have been made to believe that the Indian democracy with all the political and institutional support is functional and vibrant. Given the size of the country and the regional, class, cultural, linguistic, and religious disparities that exist, the desperate attempts by political parties to work around these factors pose a huge challenge for governance; and the biggest victim is democracy. It is an irony that a country like India which claims to have had democratic institutions even in the Vedic period (more than 3,000 years back)[1] should be ranked 51 in the Democracy Index by the Economist Intelligence Unit. That rank fell 10 places in the recent report.[2]

The US Department of State's Bureau of International Information Programs has, in its essay on 'Defining Democracy,'[3] very succinctly explained a complex political phenomenon that deals with the institutionalisation of freedom; the text reads as:

> Democracy may be a word familiar to most, but it is a concept still misunderstood and misused in a time when totalitarian regimes and military dictatorships alike have attempted to claim popular support by pinning democratic labels upon themselves. Yet the power of the democratic idea has also evoked some of history's most profound and moving expressions of human will and intellect: from Pericles in ancient Athens to Vaclav Havel in the modern Czech Republic, from Thomas Jefferson's Declaration of Independence in 1776 to Andrei Sakharov's last speech in 1989.
>
> A simplistic dictionary definition of democracy is 'a government by the people in which the supreme power is vested in the people and exercised directly by them or by their elected agents under a free electoral system'. Abraham Lincoln went on to make it even simpler and understandable for everyone in his definition of it being a government "of the people, by the people, and for the people."
>
> It is often seen that people confuse freedom with democracy and end up using these terms interchangeably. These are not synonymous. Democracy is a set of ideas and principles about freedom but converted into practices and procedures and which have evolved over time. In short, democracy is the institutionalization of freedom. For this reason, it is possible to identify the

time tested fundamentals of constitutional government, human rights and equality before the law that any society must possess to be properly called a democracy.

Democracies fall in two basic categories: direct and representative. In a direct democracy, all citizens, without the intermediary of elected or appointed officials, can participate in making public decisions. Such a system is clearly only practical with relatively small number of people, in a community organization or tribal council, for example, or a labour union, where members can meet in single room to discuss issues and arrive at decisions by consensus or majority vote. Ancient Athens, the world's first democracy managed to practice direct democracy with an assembly that may have numbered as many as 5,000 to 6,000 persons, perhaps the maximum number that could physically gather in one place and practice democracy.

Modern societies, with their size and complexities, offer few opportunities for direct democracy. Even in the Northeastern United States, where the New England town meeting is a hallowed tradition, most communities have grown too large for all the residents to gather in a single location and vote directly on issues that affect their lives.

Today, the most common form of democracy, whether for a town of 50,000 or a nation of 50 million, is representative democracy, in which citizens elect officials to make political decisions, formulate laws, and administer programs for the public good. In the name of the people, such officials can deliberate on complex public issues in a thoughtful and systematic manner that requires an investment of time and is often impractical for the vast majority of private citizens.

How such officials are elected can vary enormously. At the national level, for example, legislators can be chosen from districts that each elect a single representative. Alternatively, under a system of proportional representation, each political party is represented in the Legislature according to its percentage of the total vote nationwide. Provincial and local elections can mirror these national models, or choose their representatives more informally through group consensus instead of elections. Whatever the method used, public officials in a representative democracy hold office in the name of the people and remain accountable to the people for their elections.

Majority Rule and Minority Rights

All democracies are systems in which citizens freely make political decisions by majority rule. But, rule by majority is not necessarily democratic. No one, for example, would call a system fair or just that permitted 51 percentage of the population to oppress the remaining 49 percentage in the name of majority. In a democratic society, majority rule must be coupled with guarantee of individual human rights that, in turn, serve to protect the rights of minorities—whether ethnic, religious, or political, or simply losers in the debate over a piece of controversial legislation. The rights of minorities do not depend upon the goodwill of the majority and cannot be eliminated by majority vote. The rights of minorities are protected because democratic laws and institutions protect the rights of all citizens.

Diane Ravitch, scholar, author, and former assistant US secretary of education, wrote in a paper for an educational seminar in Poland: 'When a representative democracy operates in accordance with a constitution that limits the powers of the government and guarantees fundamental rights of all citizens, this form of government is a constitutional democracy. In such a society, the majority rules and rights of the minorities are protected by the law and through institutionalization of law'.

These elements define the fundamental elements of all modern democracies, no matter how varied in history, culture and economy. Despite their enormous differences as nations and societies, the essential elements of constitutional government—majority rule coupled with individual and minority rights, and the rule of law—can be found in Canada and Costa Rica, France and Botswana, Japan and India.

Democratic Society

Democracy is more than a set of rules and procedures that determine how a government functions. In a democracy, government is only one element coexisting in a social fabric of many and varied institutions, political parties, organisations and associations. This diversity is called pluralism, and it assumes that many organised groups and institutions in democratic society do not depend upon the government for their existence, legitimacy, or authority.

Thousands of private organisations operate in a democratic society, some local, some national. Many of them serve a mediating role between individuals and the complex social and governmental institutions of which they are a part, filling roles not given to the government, and offering individuals opportunities to exercise their rights and responsibilities as citizens of democracy.

These groups represent the interests of their members in a variety of ways, by supporting candidates for public office, debating issues, and trying to influence policy decisions. Through such groups, individuals have an avenue for meaningful participation both in government and in their own communities. The examples are many and varied: charitable organisations and churches, environmental groups, business associations and labour unions.

In authoritarian societies, virtually all such organizations would be controlled, licensed, watched, or otherwise accountable to the government. In a democracy, the powers of the government are, by law, clearly defined and sharply limited. As a result, private organisations are free of government control and, on the contrary, many of them lobby the government and seek to hold it accountable for its actions. Other groups, concerned with the art, practice of religious faiths, scholarly research, or other interests, may choose to have a little or no contact with the government at all.

In this busy private realm of democratic society, citizens can explore the possibilities of freedom and responsibilities of self government without any pressure from the potentially heavy hand of the state.

THE PILLARS OF DEMOCRACY

Sovereignty of the people.

Government based upon consent of the governed.

Majority rule.

Minority rights.

Guarantee of basic human rights.

Free and fair elections.

Equality before law.

Due process of law.

Constitutional limits on government.

Social, economic, and political pluralism.

Values of tolerance, pragmatism, cooperation and compromise.

This essay is an excellent base document and provides direction for taking the discussion forward. Democracy is a word coined by Greeks meaning 'power to people'. It is a great concept if visualised in the context of emperors, kings, monarchs and despots who have ruled and still rule the world. Democracy is an idea that when applied in its purest form provides the freedom seekers with wings to fly in pursuit of individual happiness—happiness being the ultimate aim of existence.

Athens (a Greek city-state) developed the idea of democracy around sixth century BC.[4] It is often described as the first known democracy in the world. Participation was not open to all citizens, but was instead limited to adult male citizens (not foreign residents, slaves, or women), who were no more than 30 per cent of the population.[5]

Next attempt towards empowering people was made by

a rebellious group of barons against an unpopular King John of England in the year 1215. In order to quell the rebellion and make peace with the barons, a charter of rights was agreed upon and signed by King John at Runnymede near Windsor on 15 June 1215. It promised the protection of church rights, protection of barons from illegal imprisonment, access to justice and limitation on feudal payments to the crown to be implemented through a council of 25 barons. Neither side stood by these commitments, and the charter was annulled by Pope Innocent III leading to the First Baron's War.

After the death of King John, his son Henry III reissued the document in 1216, stripped of the more radical content, in an unsuccessful bid to build political support for their cause. At the end of the war in 1217, it formed part of the peace treaty at Lambeth, where the document acquired the name MAGNA CARTA. Short of funds, Henry reissued the charter again in 1225 in exchange for a grant of new taxes. His son, Edward I, repeated the exercise in 1297, this time confirming it as a part of England's statue law. The charter became part of English political life and was typically renewed by each monarch in turn, although as time went by and the Parliament of England passed new laws, it lost some of its practical significance.[6]

Magna Carta still forms an important symbol of liberty today, and is held in 'the greatest respect by the British and American legal communities'. Lord Denning described it as "the greatest constitutional document of all times—the foundation of the freedom of individual against the arbitrary authority of the despots".

In pursuit of a democratic State, the American War of Independence occupies an important place. Attempts by the

British government to raise revenue by taxing their thirteen colonies in America, by new legislations like Stamp Act of 1765, Townshend Act of 1767 and the Tea Act of 1773 met with unexpected resistance from its citizens. They demanded representation in the British Parliament so as to be able to present their case before promulgating laws which affected the citizens of British colonies in America. Colonial resistance resulted in violence on the streets leading to British soldiers opening fire on the mob and killing five colonists. This incidence is known in history as Boston Massacre. In another incident, a group of Bostonians dressed as Mohawk Indians boarded British ships and dumped 342 chests of tea into Boston harbour during the Boston Tea Party. An outraged English parliament passed series of measures known as the Intolerable Acts or Coercive Acts designed to regain imperial authority in the region.[7]

In response, a group of colonial delegates (including George Washington, Samuel Adam, Patrick Henry and John Lay) met in Philadelphia in September 1774 to give voice to their grievances against the British Crown. This first Continental Congress did not go so far as to demand independence from Britain, but it denounced taxation without representation, as well as maintaining the British Army in the colonies without their consent. It issued a declaration of the rights of every citizen, including life, liberty, property, assembly and trial by Jury. The Continental Congress voted to meet again in May 1775 to consider further, but by that time violence had already broken out.

On the night of 18 April 1775, hundreds of British soldiers marched from Boston to nearby Concord, Massachusetts, in order to seize an arms cache. Paul Revere and other riders sounded the alarm, and colonial militiamen began mobilising to intercept the Redcoats. On 19 April, local militiamen clashed with British troops in the Battles of Lexington and Concord in Massachusetts, making the "shot heard round the world" that signified the start of the American Revolutionary War.[8]

France entered this war of independence on the side of American revolutionaries in 1778, turning the civil war into an international war. Entry of France helped the Continental Army to force the surrender at Yorktown, Virginia in 1781. Americans had effectively won their independence though fighting continued till 1783.[9]

The Peace of Paris of 1783 was a set of treaties that ended the American Revolutionary War. On 3 September 1783, representatives of King George III of Great Britain signed a treaty in Paris with representatives of the United States of America, commonly known as the Treaty of Paris (1783)—and two treaties at Versailles with representatives of King Louis XVI of France and King Charles III of Spain—commonly known as the Treaties of Versailles (1783). The treaty ending the war with Dutch Republic was signed much later on 20 May 1784.[10]

This is the story of the birth of the first great democratic republic country in the world—the United States of America. They wanted their government to be very different from the parliamentary system in UK. They opted for complete separation of power between legislators, executive and judiciary.

One wonders why India adopted Parliamentary democracy when, at the time of drafting of our Constitution, it had an established example of the very successful working of over 150 years of Presidential form of government in USA. India's need was to have tighter checks and balances to provide comfort to the minorities and the underprivileged to be able to seek and get justice as and when required. This is possible when an unambiguous and clear separation of power between Executive and the Judiciary is created. Clear separation of power between Executive and Legislature is also important to ensure that legislators do not function in connivance and collaboration with the public servants to the detriment of a minority group or groups.

In hindsight, it is felt that India would have been better served with a Presidential form of government, the type practised by USA with complete separation of power between the three arms of the government. In order to understand the minds of the people who were involved in drafting and finalising the Constitution of India, the authors decided to go through the debates of the Constituent Assembly of the sessions that were held in December 1948 for the finalisation of the draft.

The finalisation of the draft of the Indian Constitution was done by the Constituent Assembly of India, the body comprising of the members chosen by the members of the Provincial Legislative Assemblies, according to the scheme recommended by the Cabinet Mission. As per the arrangement, 292 members were elected by the Provincial Assemblies, 93 represented the Princely States and 4 represented the Chief Commissioners' Provinces. However, of the total 389 members, the strength came down to 299 after partition of the country. Jawaharlal Nehru assigned the task of drafting to the Assembly and it appointed a Drafting Committee with BR Ambedkar, KM Munshi, Mohammad Saadulla, BL Mitter, DP Khaitan, N Gopalaswami and Krishnaswami Ayyar as its members. The Committee, in its first meeting on 30 August, 1947, appointed BR Ambedkar as its Chairman.

This Committee was mandated to work on the provisional draft prepared by the Assembly's Constitutional Advisor, BN Rau. The Committee produced its draft of the proposed Constitution of India in February 1948. The draft was drawn from a number of sources. Considering India's disparate needs, its framers borrowed features from the previous legislations such as Government of India Act 1858, the India Council Acts of 1861, 1892, and 1909, the Government of India Acts 1919, and 1935 and the Indian Independence Act of 1947. It is important and significant to note that this draft was widely circulated to the members of Provincial Governments, Central Ministries, the Supreme Court, the High Courts and in the public domain for comments and suggestions. The draft was based on the Parliamentary form of government. Strangely, they did not even consider the suitability or the unsuitability of the Presidential form of government in India. It appears that there was such a strong bias against American capitalism that the members refused to even consider this form of government. Most of the members had strong socialist leanings and associated the American Presidential form of government with its capitalism.

The genesis of the decision to have a Parliamentary form of government goes back to the Government of India Act of 1919 and Government of India Act of 1935. The Act of 1919 was an Act of the Parliament of the United Kingdom. It was passed to expand participation of Indians in the government. The Act embodied the reforms recommended in the report of Secretary of State for India, Edwin Montagu, and the Viceroy, Lord Chelmsford. The Act covered validity for ten years from 1919 to 1929. It was set to be reviewed by the Simon Commission in the intervening ten years. The Act provided dual form of government for the major provinces. In each such province, control of some areas of the government, "the transferred list" was given to a Government of Ministers answerable to the Provincial Council. The transfer list included only agriculture, health and education. All other areas of governance remained with the Governor of the State. The Imperial Legislative Council was enlarged and reformed. It became a bicameral legislature for all India. The Lower House was the Legislative Assembly of 145 Members, of which 104 were elected and 41 were nominated, and the Assembly had a three year tenure. The Upper House was the Council of State, consisting of 34 elected and 26 nominated Members, with a tenure of five years. Working of the Governments in Provinces as also of the Imperial Council was based on Parliamentary Democracy.[11]

The growing demand for constitutional reforms in India by Indian leaders and India's support provided to Britain in the first world war added to the acknowledgement of the need to involve Indian leaders in the running of the Indian territory. This led to a new Government of India Act of 1935 passed by the British government. The Act was based on a white paper published by the British government in 1933 on the Simon Commission report recommendations of Round Table Conferences and the report made by the Joint Select Committee.

The new Act brought about further changes in working of the Indian government by transferring some more areas of responsibilities to the elected ministers at the provincial level as well as at the federal level. For the purpose of our discussion here, it may be mentioned that the Act was a milestone in the development of a responsible constitutional government in India. This, more or less, set the course for accepting Parliamentary form of government for Independent India without even discussing the alternative form.

Prior to 1935 Act, on 17 May 1927, at the Bombay Session of the Congress, Motilal Nehru had moved a resolution calling upon the working committee to frame a Constitution for India in consultation with the elected members of the Central and Provincial Legislators and the leaders of political parties. Based on the declaration of rights, a resolution was passed asking for *'purna swaraj'* for India The conference appointed a small committee with Motilal Nehru as its chairman and seven other members to determine the principles of the Constitution of India. The report of the committee known as 'The Nehru Report' was essentially to pressurise the British Government to allow India to have its own parliamentary democratic government under the British Crown with dominion status like Canada, Australia, New Zealand, et al, facilitating Indian citizens to have all the fundamental rights that go with democracies. This report also did not consider the viability of having a Presidential form of government.

The India Independence Act 1947 passed by the British Parliament was: a) to divide the subcontinent into two countries—India and Pakistan; b) both to be dominions of the British Crown; and c) both countries to be given the choice to become democratic republics having their own Constitution. Till then, the Viceroy was to continue holding responsibility for foreign affairs and defence of the country. The transition from the Government of India Act of 1919, to Motilal Nehru's report, to the Government of India Act 1935 and finally the India Independence Act 1947, was centered on Parliamentary democracy and not the Presidential form of government. Refusal to even consider an alternative form of government is a lapse that has had serious detrimental impact on the evolution of the Indian State.

In the Constituent Assembly Debates (CAD), KT Shah, a very learned professor and alumnus of London School of Economics, a liberal democrat and a socialist, while speaking on the subject of separation of powers between the principal organs of the state—the legislature, executive and the judiciary tried his best to convince the house to have a government free from corruption and nepotism, which protects the constitutional rights of the people both in letter and spirit. He said:

> Sir, I regard this as the most important, the very basic requirement of what I would call a liberal constitution. I am aware, Sir, that this Draft has been founded on the compromise between what are known as Presidential governments and Parliamentary governments. The Parliamentary government has a sort of link between the Executive, the Legislature and the Judiciary. The Presidential tries to keep no such link, and has complete separation of power between the three principal organs of the State, each embodying the sovereignty of the people in the different aspects of a state's activity.

He said that:

> The ideal, however, and the reasons for that ideal, which have guided many States in basing their constitution upon a doctrine of complete separation have arisen from bitter

past experience. In the Constitutions like that of England centuries ago, the ultimate combination of all authority in the person of the king, had led to many evils culminating in a civil war, ending in the execution of one king, and a bloodless revolution leading to the abdication of another. The arrangement which was evolved thereafter has been kept in conformity with the genius of the British people, not so much by a written constitution, as by evolving constitutional conventions, supported by centuries of usage. And these have become even more sacred than the written word in a written constitution.

KT Shah continuing the debate said:

But I do not think it will be applicable to us in this country. I do not think that it would be easy in new grounds, where new experiments of self-governments are being tried on an imperial scale. As such, I feel persuaded that when we start our own Constitution, when we make a beginning in this land, in the working of democracy, I think it would be best if we have complete separation of powers between the three principal organs of the government. For one thing, Sir, if you maintain the complete independence of all three, you will secure measure of independence between Judiciary, for example, and the Executive, or between the Judiciary and the Legislature. This in my view is of the highest importance in maintaining the liberty of the subject, the civil liberties and the rule of law. If there was contact between the Judiciary and the Legislature, for instance, if it was

> possible to interchange between the highest judicial officers and the membership of the Legislature, then I am afraid, the interpretation of the law will be guided much by Party influence than by intrinsic merit of each case. The Legislature in a democratic assembly is bound to be influenced by the party reasons rather than by reasons of principle.
>
> It is of utmost importance that the Judiciary be above suspicion, and, therefore, out of or above any contamination. It should be above contamination by political prejudices that are rife in all political parties. In the environment in which we are living, in the traditions under which our judicial system has been evolved, I am afraid justice is a very costly luxury. It is really not the easy privilege of the poor man. Though you have provided a number of appeals and have provided a hierarchy of powers, you have also evolved, side by side, a most costly, most wasteful, a most extravagant system of legal advice and legal assistance by professional lawyers. Only those who have undergone protracted litigation have knowledge of how costly it is, how confusing, and how almost prohibitive it is for ordinary mortals. We should have the ideal of absolute purity in justice; even though it should happen to be class justice, let us make it at least free from taint of ulterior motives.

Continuing with his argument for separation of powers of Executive and Legislature, Shah said:

> The less contact there is between them the better for

> both. The executive is in a position to corrupt the house, in a position to influence votes of the members, by the number of gifts or favours they have in their power to confer in shape of offices, in the shape of Ministerships, in the shape of Ambassadorships, in the shape of Consulships, and in any number of offices which the Executive has in its power to bestow. We have come to a stage in political evolution when the old system called the 'spoils system' is no longer upheld in any civilized country. But yet, in fact, it does happen that fifty, sixty, seventy, a hundred people may be open to be influenced by those who have it in their power to distribute even the highest office of the State (meant President). In England, for instance, out of 615 Members of Parliament, something like 70 Members are Cabinet Ministers or Parliamentary Secretaries, or other Ministers, and so on. I hope the House will pardon me for saying this—we are trying to reproduce here by creating Ministers, Minister of State and Deputy Ministers, and I suppose Parliamentary Secretaries to come. These may be, and I am sure they are, all honourable people influenced entirely by the desire of offering their services and their talent to the services of the country. But still the fact remains that the influence of the party system, the idea of one's own people, those who agree with them and become their camp-followers, is a much more influential and important consideration than the absolute and exclusive eye to the merit or the fitness or the appropriateness of an individual for an office.

Elaborating his argument in support of separation of power

between the Executive and the Legislature he continued:

> It is the exigency of the parliamentary government, as it has been developed in the West and which we are copying, that the consideration most prominent in such appointments is how many votes can an individual bring if he is appointed to a given ministerial office rather than how much real service he would be able to render to the country. As such I for one unhesitatingly and unexceptionally condemn the system of parliamentary government, the system of link between the Legislature and the Executive on which this constitution is based. I know that my voice almost appears as a voice in wilderness, but I think it my duty to place this on record. After a close study of the working of constitutions elsewhere, I venture to suggest that this is not a very healthy example we are copying and we should get rid of the combination of executive, judiciary and legislature in some supreme cabinet.

In conclusion, Shah spoke about the successful American structure of governance. He said:

> Sir, I come to the division between the Executive and Legislature. It has worked for over a hundred and fifty years in America quite satisfactorily where the Legislature and the Executive are kept wholly apart. They had before them much more than we have before us, the model of English Constitution where the combination had already been achieved to a degree of perfection that was looked

> upon even by such students as Burke or Fox as the basis of their Civil Liberties, of the liberalism of the English Constitution. Nevertheless, under the influence and aegis of scholars and thinkers of the type of Thomas Jefferson, they did devise a constitution which kept completely apart the Legislature, the Executive and the Judiciary. For a hundred and fifty years that Constitution has worked well without any serious difficulty. Even in the midst of wars, and even under internal civil war, they have been able to maintain their freedom and their liberal constitution.

Shah was not alone in arguing for complete separation of the three arms of the government. Prof Shibban Lal Saxena also had very similar views. He said:

> I agree with Mr Hanumanthaiya that the clause as it stands here in the amendment will not be in its proper place in the Constitution. Yet I cannot help saying that I agree to a very great extent with the reasoning advanced by my friend, Prof. K.T. Shah. We have experimented with the parliamentary democracy for so many years now. I personally feel that though Dr. Ambedkar in his historical address very clearly told us that we have to choose between the British system, and the American system, and said that the American system gives more security and British system more responsibility; if it were left to his choice he would have preferred the American system. I agree to a great extent about the evils of the present parliamentary system. We have seen

parliamentary parties in so many provinces like Sind, in Bengal and in other places where Ministers try to keep their parties by giving bribes to the people who have even four or five votes so that the majority party remains in being. I feel that this system wherein people have merely to keep majority in power is being put to abuse. I know that in England they are working the system in a perfect manner. But they have a tradition of 700 years. They have developed this method whereas we are just entering upon our democratic freedom and we cannot imitate England. Probably our slavery has led us to imitate the British system. If left to ourselves we would have copied the American system. In that system there is complete separation of the judicature from the legislature and the legislature from the executive.

The legislature there can pass any laws which it thinks best for the country and the President has to obey them. Here the Leader of the majority party must have the house with him. The House will only pass those laws which the party thinks are necessary. The legislature cannot be independent of, but it has to be submissive to, the executive. In most places where the leaders are outstanding, the party will say 'ditto' to what they say and the real will of the majority will not be voiced. Therefore, I think this becomes more like a one man Government than anything else. In America people are free; they can pass laws even against the President. There have been cases where in spite of laws passed by the legislature—the Congress—it has been set aside by the Supreme Court and the President has to see that any action of his is not

> against the fundamental laws of justice. The Supreme Court is far more powerful than anyone else. I, however, think that now we have gone too far to change the basis of our Constitution, because in the last two years we have passed everything in accordance with the British Constitution. But I do think that there is great force in what Prof. Shah has said and though his amendment is not in its proper place, still I do think that this House will remember that although we are for a system which has been tried in England and is working there satisfactorily, in our country we will have to be careful to develop traits which make that constitutional working possible.

Kazi Syed Karimuddin also spoke on the lines of Shah in favour of the amendments proposed by him. To highlight the points to strengthen the argument for separation of power he said: "I urge the adoption of a non-parliamentary system of government in India. We have, since 1920, seen that the working of the Government of India Act and other Local Self-governing Acts based on the parliamentary system of governance have demonstrated miserable failure. In the parliamentary system of government, it is as clear as daylight that the political opponents are practically crushed, neglected and ignored; we have no conventions and no discipline. What we have seen in India is that the Ministers are slaves of the legislature." He presented another example to drive home the point in favour of separation of power. "We have seen in the country, particularly in Noakhali, in Bihar and in the two Punjab's, arson and murder and looting. It all happened because of the governments based on parliamentary democracy."

He was clearly of the view that we should not worry about the possible conflicts at times which, according to him, were a healthy sign and not a sign of weakness in the system. Elaborating this point he said, "Sir, it was said that there would be a great conflict between the legislature, the executive and the judiciary, if there was a non-parliamentary system of government. My submission is that it will all be to the good if the judiciary is independent of the executive and disagrees with the excesses committed by the legislature. It would be a healthy sign in a democratic State. It was also said that the Ministers and the executive have to please people. Well, that is exactly the reason why we want a non-parliamentary system of government. We want separation of power between the legislature, the executive and the judiciary." He was also of the view that, "If you really want a stable and a strong government, if you really want communalism to die out, you must create an atmosphere in which popular frenzy will have no room and in which political opposition will be tolerated." He was, therefore, in favour of the amendment moved by Shah.

The other side of the aisle (represented by the opposition) had a lot many members who were not willing to concede on the point of separation of the power of executive and the legislature. BR Ambedkar, Chairman of Drafting committee, who was himself a votary of judiciary being independent of the executive, was not in favour of the executive being independent of the legislature. He mentioned:

> With regard to separation of power between Executive and Legislature, it is true that such a separation does exist in the Constitution of the United States but, if my friend,

> Prof. Shah, had read some of the recent criticism of that particular provision of the Constitution of the United States, he would have noticed that many Americans themselves were quite dissatisfied with the rigid separation embodied in the American Constitution between the executive and the legislature. One of the proposals made by some students of the American Constitution is to obviate and do away with the separation between executive and legislature completely so as to bring the position in America on the same level as, for instance, in UK. It is being advocated that the members of the executive shall be entitled to be in the House of Representatives or the Senate without participation.

He went on to add that, "There is not the slightest doubt in my mind and in the minds of many students of political science, that the work of Parliament is so complicated, so vast that unless and until the members of Legislature receive direct guidance and initiative from the members of Executive sitting in Parliament, it will be very difficult for members of Parliament to carry on the work of Legislature." In conclusion he said:

> I personally do not think there is very great loss that is likely to occur if we do not adopt the American method of separating the Executive from the Legislature. With regard to separation of Executive from the Judiciary, there is no difference of opinion and that proposition in my judgment does not depend at all on the question whether we have a Presidential form of Government or a Parliamentary form of Government. The separation of

> the Judiciary from Executive is an accepted proposition, to which we ourselves are committed by the article that we have passed, and which is now forming part of the Directive Principles, I, therefore, think that it is not possible for me to accept the amendment.

To say that the work of legislators is very complicated and requires guidance from executives is, to say the least, an exaggeration. American legislators do not require any help from their executives.

Prominent among those who were opposed to the amendment tabled by Shah and others for separation of powers between executive and legislature was K Hanumanthaiya. He said:

> Sir, I have listened with great respect to Prof. Shah's argument about his amendment. I fear the new clause he has moved is completely out of tune with the constitutional structure which this house has proposed and the Drafting Committee has adumbrated. We in this house have given our approval to the Parliamentary system of government. Of course, we can argue about the merits and the demerits of both the systems, but we have come to accept the parliamentary system to be suitable to this country for very good reasons; the system seems to be better adapted to the conditions in India than Presidential Executive. I think instead of having a conflicting trinity it is better to have a harmonious governmental structure. If we, as he says, completely separate the executive, judiciary and legislature, conflicts

> are bound to arise between these three departments of the government. In any country or in any government, conflicts are suicidal to the peace and the progress of the country. The first and foremost foundation on which a government or society can work is peace. Prof. Shah wants complete separation; then conflicts are sure to arise between these three departments. Therefore, I say that in a government structure, it is necessary to have what is called 'harmonious' rather than a three-fold conflict.

Hanumanthaiya, who continued with his theme of not wanting separation of powers between the departments of the government, said:

> It has become the fashion of the day with some people to decry the executive and make the judiciary look as if it is a paragon of all virtues. I would respectfully place this view before Prof. Shah and people of his way of thinking. Whereas judges no doubt are impartial and have no sides to take, we must remember also that the executives in governments in India or anywhere else in the world have to work under very difficult circumstances. To carry on a government and to please everyone is not an easy matter. Many a times they work under difficult circumstances with danger to their lives. They will naturally incur displeasure.

He concluded by saying that, "I oppose the new clause. My main reason is that this house is wedded to a parliamentary system of democracy and this new clause is out of place in such a constitutional structure."

Objections raised by those on the opposing side had a variety of reasons. Ambedkar's reasoning for opposing the proposal just because there were a few critics of the American system of complete separation of executive and legislature seems frivolous. Despite the criticism, the USA has not changed the system and has done phenomenally well in the little over 150 years after their independence, under their Constitution. His approach was not befitting a person of his stature or the position that he was holding in the house. He knew that his words carried a lot of weight with the members of the Assembly and that he must present all the facts in an unbiased manner to help others to take the appropriate decision. Just because there are some critics of a system does not make the system unworthy of emulation. Instead of discarding or rejecting the system, its shortcomings should have been discussed to find remedies to overcome them. Democracies, by their very nature, are not perfect. Winston Churchill was right when he said, "Democracy is the worst form of Government except for all those other forms that have been tried from time to time..." He was talking about parliamentary democracy. The reason for Ambedkar not supporting the amendment perhaps lay somewhere else.

Most others who did not support Shah's amendment felt that it was too late in the day to alter the earlier decision to stick to the parliamentary system. A few legislators declined to support because they thought the amendment that was sought was out of place so were not even willing to discuss it.

As per the proposed scheme of things, the President's position was to be pivotal in keeping the judiciary independent. Besides his responsibility to keep a watch on the functioning of the Government to see that it is working within the framework of the Constitution, he has another very important task of appointing judges of Supreme Court and High Courts. Almost all members of the Constituent Assembly were in general agreement for keeping the judiciary completely independent. If judiciary was to be independent, the authority appointing judges had to, necessarily, be independent. One should not expect the President, who is virtually a man of the party in power, to be appointing judges who may have differences with the government, particularly when dealing with cases involving government(s) as litigants. It is strange that no one, not even Ambedkar, who was in favour of complete independence of judiciary saw the importance of keeping the position of the President independent. The President, who is installed by the party in power, would have the moral obligation to go by the recommendations of the party, which in turn would exercise influence on the Judiciary for getting their favourites recommended by them. The independence of our Judiciary has been, in this process, severely compromised when deciding to elect the President through electoral college. If the President were to be elected directly through an adult franchise, he/she would be morally accountable to all the people of the country and would not come under any political influence or compulsion.

Being elected through an electoral college, the President essentially becomes a part of the party in power. If there is a change of the party in power, a shift in his loyalty is likely because of the temptation of seeking a re-election with the support of the new party in power. We seem to have landed ourselves in a situation wherein the President of India is a part of the political party in power without officially being so. The answer to this question can be found only by going back, once again, through the deliberations of the Constituent Assembly. Important deliberations on the subject took place on 13 December 1948. The debate was lengthy, covering the President's responsibilities, his status and his powers, etc. Once again, it was seen that KT Shah was the most active participant.

Debate on the subject of appointment of the President started on 10 December 1948 with KT Shah moving that Article 41 be substituted to say: 'The Chief Executive and the Head of the State in the Union of India shall be called the President of India.' In justification of his move he said, "In the title of the President, instead of the clause giving it barely as it stands, I should like that there be some indication of the status and power of the President of India whose position and title should be made a little more clear and defined than it is at present. I, therefore, describe him as 'the Chief Executive and Head of the State'." He further added that:

> I take it that there is dispute regarding the status of the President as the Head of State. That is in a way different from the Head of the Government, which may be the Prime Minister or the President himself as I had conceived it. But whether or not there is a separate Head of the Government, there must be for formal, ceremonial and solemn occasions, a representative of the people collectively embodying the sovereignty of the whole people and of the State as a whole. I think it would be better if my amendment is substituted for the original article, and the President is also described

> as the Chief Executive and Head of the State in the Union of India, called the President of India. I do not think I need to take the time of the House by dilating upon this. Therefore, without taking any further time, I commend it to the house.

Debating on the amendment of the article 41 moved by KT Shah, Mahavir Tyagi said:

> Sir, my only point is to emphasise the amendment tabled by Prof. KT Shah which points out a direction which is very important from the point of view of a discussion on the floor of this House. He says: 'the Head of the State in India represents the sovereignty of the people'. We have not yet decided the question of the residence of sovereignty. I had moved an amendment on this point and it was promised it would be taken up for consideration when we discuss the Preamble to the Constitution. I am waiting for that opportunity. Sir, I feel that Head of the State must also represent the sovereignty of the people. After all, how will otherwise the people express themselves? No Government in democratic countries can ever claim to be fully representative of the people as a whole.
>
> The Government, although they represent the ambitions and aspirations of the people and are the most popular in the country, it cannot be said that they are the representatives of the total population of India; they are not representatives of the whole people because they have a party bias and a party manifesto on which

they have been elected. The Government must as a rule represent majority party in the country. A Government cannot, therefore, be the true spokesman of the whole people. There must be some unit, some authority, some person in whom paramountcy or sovereignty should be vested, in whom the prerogatives of the people should be vested. I therefore submit, Sir, that it would have been a good idea if it had been laid down that the President was not only the Executive Head of the State but also a symbol of the sovereignty of the people. Sir, I want a distinction between the people and the State. The State has always the bias of the administration.

In the problem of governed, whether it be democracy or any other cracy, the state governs and the people are governed. It is, therefore, necessary that in a democratic State, full chance of expression should be given to the minorities or the opposition. Because, when minorities speak in the House of the Legislature or in Parliament, they speak purely with the bias of the people. In this House, as it is, if it were sitting as legislative Assembly—we are now the Constituent Assembly—Dr. Ambedkar and his colleagues would always represent the bias of the administration. They know the difficulties of administration, but the people want their own bias to be expressed of what the administrative difficulties are. Such expression and demands always come through the mouthpiece of the opposition, which has to be protected against the majority rule.

Vice President (of the House) wanted him (Mahavir Tyagi)

to explain. In response, Mahavir Tyagi said:

> I want to emphasise that it is an essential requirement of the constitution that the sovereignty of the people must be vested in some person or somebody other than Government. I only want to press the argument that the Government, however popular it may be, cannot claim to be sovereign. It would have been a good idea if the President were made a symbol of the people's will so that he could command respect and devotion from all alike. He could then stand between the people and the Government. In that case he would have the capacity not only of being the Executive Head but also of the sovereignty of the people so that in him the minorities also could find their reflection and protection. Sovereignty lies in the people, but how will it express itself? It cannot be expressed by the Government, because the Government is not the total people. Sometimes, it may be majority of only fifty-one per cent and it may also be possible that a forty-nine per cent minority go unrepresented altogether. If the House agrees to vest the paramountcy and all prerogative and sovereignty in the people, then there must be some authority wherefrom the sovereignty may flow and express.

Shri K Santhanam, expressing his point of view on the subject said, "On a point of information, Sir, in this Constitution, Parliament is the repository of the sovereignty of the people. That is the scheme of all constitutions where we have the Parliamentary executive".

Mahavir Tyagi responded by saying:

> My friend has taken me aback. I cannot immediately reply to his argument, but I feel that sovereignty will not be represented by the Parliament because the Parliament also includes the Council of Sates which is not representative of the people because as envisaged here, the Council of States will be the representative only of the majority parties in the provinces. That House will not come through the single transferable vote system of the proportional representation; it will be a House of the States and the members thereof must represent the various States which in turn are again the representatives of the majority party. In these circumstances, the members of the Upper House will be representatives of their Government and not of the people. There are to be 250 members of the Council of States. They will always be biased by the difficulties of Government in the various States. They will come here to represent their Governmental difficulties and to pose their demands from the point of view of their governments.

Addressing the Vice President of the House, he continued:

> I am aware of your anxiety to finish the discussion early. Sir, my friend TT Krishnamachari says that as the members of the Council of States will also be elected by the elected representatives of the people, they will represent the people. I claim they will not. For instance I have been elected by the people in my province as an

> M.C.A. but if I am deputed to be on the Public Service Commission, certainly in the Commission I shall act purely as a member of the Commission; I will not use my capacity as a representative. Likewise, when you elect members to the Council of States, they cannot use their representativeship of the people; they will represent their respective States. They are deputed to represent their governments. I, therefore, submit that the Parliament will not be so ideal a representative of the people's sovereignty, as the Parliament will always be run by the majority party. If those who are governed cannot express themselves directly, then let their mouthpiece, the President, speak for them and let him guard the interest of the minorities and, also, of the people as a whole. I submit, Sir, it is a question which warrants deep consideration. I, therefore, hope that the House will give due consideration to the suggestion made.

On the question of amendment raised by KT Shah, Ambedkar said:

> I come to the question raised substantially by the amendment of Prof. KT Shah. His amendment, if I understand him correctly, is fundamentally different from the whole scheme as has been adopted in the Draft Constitution. Prof. KT Shah uses the words 'Chief Executive and the Head of the State'. I have no doubt that what he means by the introduction of these words is to introduce the American Presidential form of executive and not the Parliamentary form of executive

which is contained in this Draft Constitution. If my friend Prof Shah were to turn to the report of the Union Constitution Committee he will see that the Drafting Committee has followed the proposals set out in the report of the Committee. The report of the committee says that while the President is to be head of the executive, he is to be guided by the Council of Ministers whose advice shall be binding upon him in all actions that he is supposed to take under the power given to him by the Constitution. He is not to be the absolute supreme head, uncontrolled by the advice of anybody, and that is the Presidential form of government in the United States.

Undoubtedly, there are various Secretaries of State in charge of the various departments of administration of the United States, and they carry on the administration. I have no doubt that they can also, and do as a matter of fact, tender advice to the President with regard to matters arising under their administration. All the same, in theory, the President is not bound to accept the advice of Secretaries of State. That is why the United States President is described as the Chief Head of the Executive. We have not adopted that system. We have adopted the Parliamentary system, and therefore my submission at this stage is that this matter which has been raised by Prof. KT Shah cannot be disposed of unless we first dispose of article 61 of the Draft Constitution which makes it obligatory upon the President to act upon the advice of the Council of Ministers. Do we want to say it or not, that the President shall be bound

> by the advice of his Ministers? That is the whole question. If we decide that the President shall not be bound by the advice of the Council of Ministers, then, of course, it would be possible for this House to accept the amendment of Prof. KT Shah. But my submission is that at this stage, the matter is absolutely premature. If we accept the deletion of article 61, then I agree that we would be in a position to make such consequential changes as to bring in line with the suggestion of Prof. Shah. But at this moment, I am quite certain that it is premature and should not be considered.

Amendment tabled by KT Shah, "That for article 41, the following should be substantiated: 'The Chief Executive and Head of the State in the Union of India shall be called the President of India'."

The motion was negatived when put to vote. The other issues raised by Shah and Mahavir Tyagi continued to remain on the table for further debate.

Shah moved another proposal to amend Article 43 to read as follows: "The President shall be elected by the adult citizens of India, voting by secret ballot, in each constituent part of the union." The original article provides for the election of the President by an electoral college consisting of the members of the Central Legislative, as well as those of the Provincial or the State Legislatures. He added that, "I think this is not sufficiently representative of the people's will; and as such I, at least, am persistent enough to insist upon the people's will being always held supreme." He added, "I have felt it necessary that at every point, wherever I can help it, the sovereign people shall come in, whether you like it or not, and that the people's will be asserted, whether you like it or not. I therefore suggest that every citizen shall have his share in electing the head of the state instead of indirect election through the representatives of the legislators."

He argued:

> The discussions held fourteen to fifteen months ago on the general principles of the Constitution when we decided upon what are called the leading principles, and nothing more than the leading principles, we were under stress and strain. We were passing through difficult circumstances which I venture to submit, deflected our judgement, were unbalanced and therefore, we voted for and accepted ideas, which in my opinion, were not then, and are not now consistent with the idea of a true, real, working democracy, in every sphere of life. After fifteen months we are now in a position to take a more sober, balanced, and impartial view of the situation. As such if we are true to our ideals, if we are true to the principles which we have proclaimed from the housetop, if we are true to our slogans on which we asked the old imperialist regime to quit and yield place to the children of the soil—I put it to you sir, that there is nothing improper, there is nothing out of the way for me to put before the house this amendment. It is after all for the house to judge. I only want to submit to the house the considerations on which it can accept my point of view.

He further argued:

> We should arm the President with the authority to say that he represents the people. It is no use telling him that there may be conflict between the Prime Minister or the majority party in the house and the President elected by the people. If avoiding conflict is the main objective, the President will function only in an emergency; he will function not ornamentally only but in a representative capacity with the representative of another country. Accordingly this argument would seem to be puerile namely, that you want the President to be a sort of mere gramophone of the Prime Minister. I want the President to be the head of State and representative of the people in their collective capacity and in their sovereignty. For this reason I hold that the President not be a creature of the party majority in the centre or the local legislators but a real representative of the people. In this view I may say that the possibility of conflict between the ministry and the head of the State, or other difficulties are, in my opinion, a matter of detail, which, given good sense, loyalty to the central theme of the Constitution, given sincerity amongst you the makers of the constitution, may be easily solved. I take the view that you will do very well to have the President elected by the adult vote, instead of by an indirect roundabout method.

BR Ambedkar had his own views which differed from those of Shah. Elaborating his point of view, he said:

> Sir, turning to the general debate on this article, the most important amendment is the amendment of Prof. Shah, which proposes that the President should be elected directly by adult suffrage. This matter, in my judgement, requires to be considered from three points of view. First of all, it must be considered from the size of the electorate. Let me give the house figures of the total electorate that would be involved in the election of the President, if we accept Prof. Shah's suggestion. So far as the figures are available, the total population of the Governors' provinces and the Commissioners' provinces is about 228,163,637. The total population of the States comes to 88,808,434, making altogether a total of 317 million for the territory of India. Assuming that on adult franchise, the population that would be entitled to take part in the election of President would be about 50 per cent of the population—158.5 million. Let me give the figures of the electorate that is involved in the election of the American President. The total electorate, as I understand—I speak subject to correction—is about 75 million. I think if the honourable Members will bear in mind the figure which I have given— namely 158.5 million, they would realize the impossibility of an election in which 158.5 million people would have to take part. The size of the electorate, therefore, in my judgement forbids our adopting adult suffrage in the matter of the election of the President.

The second question he wanted the Members to consider was the question of adult suffrage. This also revolved around the number of people who would be entitled to vote for electing the President. He felt that the country would not have the staff to handle this size of electorate. He also doubted there would be many candidates who would come forward to contest. He thought neither the government of India nor the state governments would be able to manage the size of the electorate. His third reason for being against the amendment tabled by Shah was that our President cannot be compared with the President of America. He argued that if a comparison was to be made, we have to compare the American President with our Chief Executive and we have our Prime Minister in the same position.

In conclusion he said:

> Having regard to the fact to which I have referred that the President has really no power to execute, the last argument which one could advance in favour of the proposition that the President should be elected by adult suffrage seems to me to fall on the ground. I, therefore, submit that, having regard to the size of the electorate, the paucity of administrative machinery to manage election on such a vast scale and that the President does not possess any of the executive administrative powers which the President of the United States does, I submit that it is unnecessary to go into the question of adult suffrage and to provide the election on that bases. Our proposal in the Draft Constitution, in my judgement is sufficient for the necessities of the case. We have provided that he shall be elected by the elected

members of the States, who themselves are elected on adult suffrage. He is also to be elected by both houses of the Parliament. The lower house of the Parliament is also elected directly by the people on the adult suffrage. The upper chamber is elected by the lower houses of the State Legislatures which are also elected on adult suffrage; therefore, having regard to these provisions, I think that Prof KT Shah's amendment is quite out of place. I, therefore, oppose that amendment.

K T Shah said:

"Mr Vice President, I beg to move that for clause (1) of article 42, the following be substituted:

1. The sovereign executive power and authority of the Union shall be vested in the President, and shall be exercised by him in accordance with the Constitution and in accordance with the laws made thereunder and in force for the time being. Or alternatively,
2. The executive authority, power and functions of Government shall be vested in the President and shall be exercised by him in accordance with the Constitution and the law with the advice and help of such ministers, officers or servants of the State as may be deemed necessary by him.

He went on to add that:

Before explaining the difference that there is between two

alternative forms of the same idea, I should like to point out, if I may, that the argument which has been urged by the Chairman of the Drafting Committee about the appropriate place of any amendment or alteration suggested in this House is a little out of place itself. The reason is that after all this is an order settled by the Drafting Committee, and we can only give amendments on the order as it is. An argument was also urged that if (and I agree with it), we go on holding discussions over amendments and articles, their mutual correlation may be forgotten or overlooked and, therefore, it would be safest perhaps, and in the best interests of all that a definite order is established. We submit most cheerfully to the suggestion you gave, at the very outset of the debate on an article that some stated amendments would be taken up and in the stated order.

That is a perfectly reasonable and proper thing to do, but when an amendment or article is placed before the House, and then suddenly a surprise is sprung upon Members that this is out of place or out of time, I think it is somewhat unfair. Let those who are responsible for drafting make up their mind in what order they will take chapter by chapter, and we can understand that and shall co-operate. The idea that we will, in the middle of discussions, switch over from one article to another or one section to another makes it, I submit in all humility, a little difficult for those who are responsible for a number of amendments to keep track, and to marshal their own arguments. One comes prepared for a particular set of articles; and one is suddenly told that they are not to be taken up or that it is not their place and

> so on. However much one may carry one's own argument in one's head, one feels a little upset to be asked all of a sudden to make up one's mind whether this thing is to be moved or not to be moved.
>
> Secondly, having moved, the argument or suggestion that this is not the proper place etc. and that a given amendment be taken after another article has been dealt with is, again I submit, a little difficult for members, because it might, so to say, prejudge the main issue. If you hold it over and get to the later article....

Vice-President: "Are you not moving my amendment Prof Shah?"

KT Shah said:

> I am placing my difficulty because the same argument may be used here again that this is out of place. That is why I am replying to it. I am very much afraid having heard this line of reasoning. I do not say that the reasoning is false; I am only saying that it makes it difficult for us to put forward, in the only way in which we can put forward, the amendments, namely, according to the order prescribed or given in the book.
>
> Having said this, I would like to point out quite frankly that naturally all my amendments hang together, and that they arise out of a certain view of the Constitution, out of certain view of the distribution of powers, of finances etc. which may not be accepted but which nevertheless is a possible, a known alternative way of doing it.

I have, therefore, brought forward this amendment. I trust it will be examined or dealt with on its merits, and not merely on the ground that it is out of place or it cannot now be discussed. I venture to submit that even if the basic principle is other than I thought would be acceptable to the House, even then, on a point like this, the powers and place of the President may be considered quite irrespective of the governing or basic principle; and if adopted, can be fitted even in the scheme of the Constitution which you have accepted.

I would, therefore, suggest that the powers and functions of the President should have the place as if they are the powers and functions of the sovereign people being exercised by the Chief Executive of the State. He will be the Chief Executive, I take it, for the time that he is in office, just as the King of England is the Chief Executive, even though the powers are not so thoroughly separated in the British Constitution as they are in the American Constitution.

I, therefore, put forward this point No.1 that it would be no answer to my amendment to say that it is not in harmony with the basic principle of this Constitution namely, that of the Parliamentary government, and not of the Presidential kind and as such it need not be discussed. I submit that it can be very well fitted in even in the terminology I have used with the basic idea of the Constitution that you have accepted, even though I am free to admit my own conception was slightly different.

To proceed, Sir, I would like the President's powers to be very clearly defined, and be exercisable in accordance with the Constitution. I take it there is no question on that. No one will say that the President is supra-Constitution. The President is a creature of the Constitution, and must work under the Constitution. No further words are, therefore, necessary to explain that emphasis which should be—in fact, it is there in the main clause.

The next point is that it must be in accordance with the laws made thereunder. Now, in a variety of articles you have given power to Parliament to make laws. If the laws are made under the Constitution, which allow or explain or expand the powers given to the several organs of Government, then it is quite in order to suggest that they should be in accordance with the laws made thereunder.

Last comes advice—the advice of the Ministers, officers and servants of the Union. I think that also is important to include in the position of the President as it is. Later on, I have tried to elaborate this point in a subsequent amendment which I shall deal with when I come to it.

In this case, however, I want that my suggestion should not be merely thrown overboard because it is inconsistent with the basic principle adopted in drafting this Constitution. I have tried to harmonise the Ministerial responsibility—I mean the doctrine of Ministerial responsibility with also the position of the President as the head of the State and Chief Executive. I once more take the analogy of the King of England, who has to act on the advice of the Ministers. At least that is the constitutional position. Every Act begins with: 'let it be enacted by the King's Most Excellent Majesty, with the advice of the Lords Spiritual and Temporal and the Commons'. Every

> action is the action of His Majesty in each particular matter as advised by the particular Minister. The whole doctrine that 'the King can do no wrong' loses its import if the doctrine of ministerial advice and ministerial responsibility is not there. I have, therefore, laid it down by this amendment, that the President must act in accordance with the Constitution and in accordance with the laws made therein and according to the advice of his ministers.

He further said:

> The addition of the 'officers and servants of State' I have felt also necessary to be quite clearly expressed in the Constitution. The President should be entitled not merely to listen to all that the Minister alone says to him; he must have power to consult any other expert, or any other officer, or servant of the State in India who may give him his views. I certainly think that it would do no harm to the working of the constitutional machinery if the President is entitled, as a matter of right, to send for any expert officer, and ask his advice, say, for example, the Attorney-General or the Advocate-General, should the President have a legal doubt with regard to his own position, vis-a-vis his own Ministers.
>
> He should be entitled, I submit, as head of the State and responsible person, to know what the expert in the department thinks. Under the parliamentary party system it will not be his veto and he would have no right to discard the advice of his Minister. The Minister's

advice will eventually prevail. But it will prevail only after the President has drawn attention to the other aspects of the matter which the Minister has overlooked, or ignored.

I am not suggesting that he should be free to go outside the country for such advice. I am not suggesting that he should invite foreign experts to advise him. He should be entitled to seek advice from his Ministers in the first place: then from the officers and from the servants of the State. This I think is in perfect harmony even if you conceive and take this Constitution to be on the principle of Ministerial responsibility, and so perfectly proper to accept it. I, therefore, commend this motion to the House.

(Amendment No. 1044 was not moved.)

K T Shah said, Mr Vice-President, I move:

That for clause (2) of article 42, the following be substituted:

(2) Without prejudice to the generality of the foregoing provision and in accordance with this Constitution and the laws made thereunder for the time being in force, the President shall:

(a) Convene or dissolve the Legislature of the Union, and place before it any proposal for legislation or for sums of money needed for the good government and efficient administration of the country, or for its defense, or to provide for any sudden calamity in any part of the Union or any other emergency;

(b) Have the power to assent to the laws duly passed by the Union Legislature;

(c) Conduct and supervise any Referendum that may be decided upon to make to the Sovereign People in accordance with this Constitution;

(d) Have the power to declare war, and make peace;

(e) Be the supreme commander of all the armed forces of the Union;

(f) Appoint all other executive and judicial officers, including the ministers, representatives of the Union in foreign countries as ambassadors, ministers, consuls, trade commissioners and the like as well as the commanding officers in the armed forces of the Union;

(g) Do all acts, exercise all powers and discharge all authority necessary or incidental to the power and authority vested in him by and under this Constitution;

(h) Have power to refuse assent to any legislative proposal passed by both Houses of Parliament or to recommend to Parliament that any legislative proposal passed by Parliament be reconsidered for reasons stated by the President, provided that any legislative proposal duly passed by Parliament, if refused assent by the President only once; that the same proposal if passed in an identical form by Parliament in the next following sessions of that body, shall be deemed to have been duly passed and become an Act of the Legislature, notwithstanding that the President has refused or continues to refuse to assent thereto;

(i) In every case in which the President refuses to assent to any legislative proposal duly passed by Parliament, the

President shall record his reasons for refusing to assent and shall forward the reasons thus recorded to Parliament; (j) In any case where the President, having duly submitted to Parliament, or to the People's House thereof, a legislative proposal he deems necessary for the safety of the State, its integrity or defence or to safeguard the nation's interests in a national emergency, finds that Parliament is unwilling to consider or pass that proposal, may refer such a proposal to the people of the country; and if the proposal is approved, on such reference, by a majority of not less than two-thirds of the citizens voting, it shall forthwith become a law of the land. If on such reference the proposal is not approved by the requisite majority, it shall be deemed to have been negatived, and shall be treated as void and have no effect.

KT Shah continued:

I come next to the question of the right to refuse assent. It may seem as if it was an innovation of my own. I do not think it is an innovation, because, technically at any rate, in the model on which this Constitution is based or appears to be made—that of the United Kingdom, the King's veto is not abolished, as the veto of the House of Lords for instance is modified. There are a number of conventions which have for centuries past guided the ministers and the people in dealing with any exercise of royal authority whether by prerogative or otherwise which does not infringe the spirit, if not the letter of the Constitution as well.

Here, however, we are making a new Constitution, and we are starting upon a new democratic career on a very large national scale. After all, you must remember that the United Kingdom compared to India is perhaps not one-tenth or one-twelfth in size; and, in point of population, it is perhaps one-sixth or one-fifth in strength of numbers. Therefore, what may have suited that country and its ways may not suit us. At any rate, they have a long history of precedents and conventions behind them. We have to make those precedents and conventions. I therefore submit it would be as well for us not to leave any room for doubt, and make precise and explicit the powers that we are vesting in the President. The right to give assent carries with it the right to refuse assent, unless you positively state that the President will not be able to refuse assent. In my amendment I have, however, laid down the conditions under which the right to refuse assent may be safeguarded. The right to refuse assent is given only once. In spite of the refusal, if Parliament proceeds with the legislation in identical form, whether or not the President agrees, it will become law. The privileges of the President, according to my amendment, only lie in his stating the reason for refusing his assent. Being popularly elected, as I conceive it, he is bound, in his sense of true responsibility to the people, as their representative to voice reasons which have actuated him in refusing assent. I do not think there is anything revolutionary in making such a suggestion. The second innovation is in regard to reference to the people, or Referendum. Now, this Constitution does not provide for reference to the people, notwithstanding the fact that we talk again and again of the people's sovereignty, of the people being the ultimate sovereign of this country. Our regard for reference to the people, or consultation with the people, is expressed, if at all, only in a quinquennial election, a general election to Parliament. In a general election, however, so many issues are mixed up; so many cross-currents take place; so many moves and counter-moves happen that the consultation with the people or the verdict of the people on such variety of issues is only nominal, if I may say so without any disrespect.

If you seriously and sincerely desire that the people shall be sovereign, if you want that the people be consulted in any emergency when your two organs of power, the Legislature and the Executive, are unable to agree, then the test will lie in your readiness to consult the people. It may be that the emergency may be so momentous that you cannot dissolve Parliament. It may be that the state of emergency may be such that the President cannot retire, and will not tender his resignation. Or it may be only a matter involving such strong difference of opinion that neither is prepared to yield. At that moment it is but right that the view of the people should be ascertained on the specific single issue worded so as to admit of a categorical answer, 'Yes' or 'No'.

Surely the test of this Constitution enshrining the sovereignty of the people is not merely the lip-loyalty that seems to be very common in this Draft. The argument could be urged, and was urged by those who were against people's sovereignty in fact and in name, that the people are not ready; or that they are not educated enough to give any decisive opinion on such complicated issues of foreign or local policy. I trust that in this House, we shall not hear such an argument. Backward as we may be—only ten or twelve per cent of us may be literate— whatever may be our deficiency or handicaps, I take it that we are all sincere, true in our belief that ultimately the people are sovereign. Where there is collective wisdom, there is after all real salvation. Vox popular vex Dei—the voice of the people is the voice of God.

That, I take it, is not merely a figure of speech, is not merely a maxim used to hypnotise children, but is intended for serious legislators to take into account and act up to it. I invite you, therefore, with all the earnestness I command to consider this matter seriously. If you think that you will take counsel together, on this amendment before giving a positive decision, here at least I am agreeable over this amendment. But I beg of you with all the earnestness at my command that, if you are sincere in your desire to make the people truly sovereign, if you want them to be trained in the art of working democracy, if you desire that they shall be the final arbiters on all issues, then for goodness' sake, do not treat this with your Party label of opposition, right or wrong.

I have not conceived my role in this House as a cussed opposition, to oppose things on every ground and on any ground. I take myself to be a friendly critic, always ready

> to offer constructive views with such brains or such ability as I have. It may be that they do not appeal to you for one reason or another. But here is a case in which I venture to submit that, if you really believe in the sovereignty of the people, if you honestly believe that the people are the true masters of our destiny, you cannot shirk this amendment. Do not decline it on merely technical grounds of its being not in proper time or place or out of place and such other camouflage. Let me also point out that I have not omitted to put in certain conditions and safeguards, so that if and when you consult the sovereign people you will not merely have a chance decision, but the considered opinion of real majority of our voters. In that case, even if the decision is wrong, we shall all be in the same boat. It is far better to sink with our fellows than swim with our masters.

(Amendment No. 1050 was not moved). The Vice-President said, "The article is open for general discussion."

RK Sidhwa said:

> Mr Vice-President, Sir, I closely followed the amendment moved by my honourable friend, Prof KT Shah, and also listened to his speech with rapt attention. I give credit for his tenacity for bringing in his viewpoint by various ways in this House, and to see that they are implemented by changing the very fundamentals of this Constitution from time to time. In this amendment that he has proposed, Sir, it will be seen that many of the clauses refer to the fundamental changes, and some of them, of

course, could be provided in the rules and regulations to be made after the Constitution comes into force. But that apart, Sir, I will presently show to this House how some of the suggestions that he has made in this amendment may be commendable for acceptance if a different type of Constitution were to be framed. But the fact is that we have taken a decision on a democratic parliamentary system of Government and if his proposal is accepted, it cannot fit in or suit the provisions we have provided in the Constitution.

For instance, in his amendment, Prof Shah says: The President shall place before the Legislature of the Union any proposal for legislation or for sums of money needed for the good government and efficient administration of the country. He wants that the President should be empowered with those powers. I want to know, Sir, how it would fit in with an Executive responsible to the Legislature, if the power of spending of money is vested in the President. It is the very negation of the very fundamental principle that we have accepted after a long discussion of five days in the opening session of this Constituent Assembly.

Then he went on to add:

Our Constitution has provided power to the President for emergency purposes, but may I know, Sir, in a responsible Legislature does Prof. Shah want the powers to declare war or peace to be entrusted absolutely to the President? Even in a responsible parliamentary

Government that will be certainly most objectionable. If a war has to be declared, the President will certainly have the power; he is the supreme head of Defence under our Constitution, but the House has to be taken into confidence. The Government has to consider this point. Suppose this clause is passed, and some autocratic President says, 'I want to declare a war in view of some exigencies arising here or around our country'. Would this be called a responsible Government? Absolutely not, Sir.

Then in clause (h) of his amendment he says that when both Houses of Parliament pass the bills, they go to the President. That is understandable. Again they come before the House and then with a certain majority he wants those bills to be passed. There may not be a very serious objection to that, but I find Sir, if his clause is accepted, there would be a deadlock always between the President's action and the Parliament. If all these clauses are finalised, there will be nothing but chaos between the Government and the President and who would like, Sir, the President being entrusted with the powers of the Executive? Certainly, we do not want them.

KM Munshi said:

Mr Vice-President, Sir, the previous speakers have already drawn attention to the fact that the amendments moved by my honourable friend Prof Shah not only to this article, but to the subsequent articles, create a fundamental change in the whole structure of the

Constitution that this House has envisaged for the last year and a quarter. At the earlier stage of the Union Constitution Committee, it was decided, I think possibly with one or two dissident voices, that our Central Government should be based on the English model and that the American model or rather the model of the United States of America was to be rejected for two valid reasons. The two issues that have been before the House and the several Committees were these: what would make for the strongest executive consistent with a democratic constitutional structure; the second is which is the form of executive best suited to the conditions of this country. I fail to see how from any of these points of view, the amendments of my honourable friend can find favour with this House.

Apart from that, the second issue which the House has to consider is—what is the best form suited to Indian conditions. We must not forget a very important fact that during the last 100 years, the Indian public life has largely drawn upon the traditions of the British Constitutional law. Most of us, and during the last several generations before us, public men in India have looked up to the British model as the best. For the last thirty or forty years, some kind of responsibility has been introduced in the governance of this country. Our Constitutional traditions have become parliamentary and we have now all our provinces functioning more or less on the British model. As a matter of fact, today, the Dominion Government of India is functioning as a full-fledged Parliamentary Government. After this experience why should we go back upon the tradition that has been built for over 100 years, and try a novel experiment which was, as said, framed 150 years ago and which has been found wanting even in America? I, therefore, submit that from this point of view the whole scheme put forward by the various amendments of Prof. Shah has not been accepted by the House so far, has not yielded the best possible result elsewhere and is against the tradition which has been built-up in India. Therefore, I submit, Sir, that the amendment should be rejected.

Alladi Krishnaswami Ayyar said:

Mr Vice-President, Sir, Prof. Shah's amendment, if it meets with the acceptance of the House, would mean that the House, for the reasons which Prof. Shah has assigned, is going back upon the decision reached by various Committees of this House as well as by the Constituent Assembly after considerable deliberation on previous occasions.

Apart from this question that it will involve going back upon the decision solemnly reached, there are weighty reasons why what may be called the Cabinet type of Government should be preferred in this country to what is generally known as the Presidential type of Government. In the first place the idea is to take the various units and provinces and the States into the Federation. There is at present no idea of effacing the rulers from the various States. What are we going to do in the case of the States if you are going to have what is called the Presidential system at the Centre? Does it mean that in the States the rulers will again be invested with real executive power and the legislatures be confined purely to their legislative functions? It will be against the marked tendency of the times. It will create insuperable difficulties in the Indian States. That is one point which may be considered.

B R Ambedkar said:

I am sorry I cannot accept any of the amendments that have been moved. So far as the general discussion of the clause is concerned, I do not think I can usefully add anything to what my friends Mr Munshi and Shri Alladi Krishnaswamy Ayyar have said.

Mr. Vice-President: I am putting the amendments one by one to vote. First part of No. 1040. The question is: That for clause (1) of article 42, the following be substituted:

(1) The sovereign executive power and authority of the Union shall be vested in the President, and shall be exercised by him in accordance with the Constitution and in accordance with the laws made thereunder and in force for the time being.

The motion was negatived.

Mr. Vice-President: I put the second part of No.1040. The question is: That for clause (1) of article 42, the following be substituted:

The executive authority, power and functions of

Government shall be vested in the President, and shall be exercised by him in accordance with the Constitution and the law with the advice and help of such ministers, officers or servants of the State as may be deemed necessary for him."

The motion was negatived.

Mr. Vice-President: I put amendment No. 1045. The question is: That for clause (2) of article 42, the following be substituted:

(2) Without prejudice to the generality of the foregoing provision and in accordance with this Constitution and the laws made thereunder for the time being in force, the President shall:

(a) Convene or dissolve the Legislature of the Union, and place before it any proposal for legislation or for sums of money needed for the good government and efficient administration of the country, or for its defence, or to provide for any sudden calamity in any part of the Union or any other emergency;

(b) Have the power to assent to the laws duly passed by the Union Legislature;

(c) Conduct and supervise any Referendum that may be decided upon to make to the Sovereign People in accordance with this Constitution;

(d) Have the power to declare war, and make peace;

(e) Be the supreme commander of all the armed forces of the Union;

(f) Appoint all other executive and judicial officers, including the ministers, representatives of the Union in foreign countries as ambassadors, ministers, consuls, trade commissioners and the like; as well as the commanding officers in the armed forces of the Union;

(g) Do all acts, exercise all powers and discharge all authority necessary or incidental to the power and authority vested in him by and under this Constitution;

(h) Have power to refuse assent to any legislative proposal passed by both Houses of Parliament; or to recommend to Parliament that any legislative proposal passed by Parliament be reconsidered for reasons stated by the President, provided that any legislative proposal duly passed by Parliament, if refused assent by the President only once; and that the same proposal if passed in an identical form by Parliament in the next following sessions of that body, shall be deemed to have been duly passed and become an Act of the Legislature, notwithstanding that the President has refused or continues to refuse to assent thereto;

(i) In every case in which the President refuses to assent to any legislative proposal duly passed by Parliament, the President shall record his reasons for refusing to assent and shall forward the reasons thus recorded to Parliament;

(j) In any case where the President, having duly submitted to Parliament, or to the People's House thereof, a legislative proposal he deems necessary for the safety of the State, its integrity or defence or to safeguard the nation's interests in a national emergency, finds that Parliament is unwilling to consider or pass that proposal, may refer such a proposal to the people of the country; and if the proposal is approved, on such reference, by a majority of not less than two-thirds of the citizens voting, it shall forthwith become a law of the land. If on such reference the proposal is not approved by the requisite majority, it shall be deemed to have been negatived, and shall be treated as void and have no effect.

The motion was negatived.

Mr. Vice-President: I now put No. 1048 to vote. The question is: That for sub-clause (a) of clause (3) of article 42, the following be substituted:

(a) Be deemed to authorise or empower the President to exercise any power or perform any function which by any existing law is exercisable or performable by the Government of any State or by any other authority;

The motion was negated.

Mr. Vice-President: Now the question is: That article 42 stand part of the Constitution.

The motion was adopted.

Article 42 was added to the Constitution.

Article 43, as amended, was added to the Constitution.

Mr. Vice-President: With the permission of the House, I should like to revert to an article left over: that is article 15. I have before me the proceedings of the House from which it appears that this was considered on 6 December. The general discussion had concluded and I had called upon Dr. Ambedkar to reply. At that time it was suggested that efforts should be made to arrive at some kind of understanding so that those who had submitted certain amendments might feel satisfied. I do not know the position now; but we cannot wait any longer. Dr. Ambedkar, will you please make the position clear? If no understanding has been arrived at, I would ask you to reply.

BR Ambedkar added:

Mr Vice-President, I must confess that I am somewhat in a difficult position with regard to article 15 and the amendment moved by my friend Pandit Bhargava for the deletion of the words 'procedure according to law' and the substitution of the words 'due process'.

It is quite clear to anyone who has listened to the debate that has taken place last time that there are two sharp points of view. One point of view says that 'due process of law' must be there in this article; otherwise the article is a nugatory one. The other point of view is that the existing phraseology is quite sufficient for the purpose. Let me explain what exactly 'due process' involves.

The question of 'due process' raises, in my judgment, the question of the relationship between the Legislature and the Judiciary. In a federal constitution, it is always open to the Judiciary to decide whether any particular law passed by the Legislature is ultra vires or intra vires in reference to the powers of legislation which are granted by the Constitution to the particular Legislature. If the law made by a particular Legislature exceeds the authority of the power given to it by the Constitution, such law would be ultra vires and invalid. That is the normal thing that happens in all federal constitutions.

Every law in a federal constitution, whether made by the Parliament at the Centre or made by the Legislature of a State, is always subject to examination by the

Judiciary from the point of view of the authority of the Legislature making the law. The 'due process' clause, in my judgment, would give the Judiciary the power to question the law made by the Legislature on another ground. That ground would be whether that law is in keeping with certain fundamental principles relating to the rights of the individual. In other words, the Judiciary would be endowed with the authority to question the law not merely on the ground whether it was in excess of the authority of the Legislature, but also on the ground whether the law was a good law, apart from the question of the powers of the Legislature making the law. The law may be perfectly good and valid so far as the authority of the Legislature is concerned. But, it may not be a good law, that is to say, it violates certain fundamental principles; and the Judiciary would have that additional power of declaring the law invalid. The question which arises in considering this matter is this. We have no doubt given the Judiciary the power to examine the law made by different legislative bodies on the ground whether that law is in accordance with the powers given to it. The question now raised by the introduction of the phrase 'due process' is whether the Judiciary should be given the additional power to question the laws made by the State on the ground that they violate certain fundamental principles.

There are two views on this point. One view is that the Legislature may be trusted not to make any law which would abrogate the fundamental rights of man, so to say, the fundamental rights which apply to every individual, and consequently, there is no danger arising from the introduction of the phrase `due process'. Another view is that it is not possible to trust the Legislature. The Legislature is likely to err, is likely to be led away by passion, by party prejudice, by party considerations, and it may make a law which may abrogate what may be regarded as the fundamental principles which safeguard the individual rights of a citizen.

We are, therefore, placed in two difficult positions. One is to give the Judiciary the authority to sit in judgment over the will of the Legislature and to question the law made by the Legislature on the ground that it is not a good law, in consonance with fundamental principles. Is that a desirable principle? The second position is that the Legislature ought to be trusted not to make bad laws. It is very difficult to come to any definite conclusion. There are dangers on both sides. For myself, I cannot altogether omit the possibility of Legislature packed by party men making laws which may abrogate or violate what we regard as certain fundamental principles affecting the life and liberty of an individual. At the same time, I do not see how five or six gentlemen sitting in the Federal or Supreme Court examining laws made by the Legislature, by dint of their own individual conscience or their bias or their prejudices, are trusted to determine which law is good and which law is bad. I would leave it to the House to decide anyway it likes.

Mr Vice-President: I shall now put the amendments one by one to vote. No. 523.The question is:

"That in article 15, for the words 'No person shall be deprived of his life or personal liberty except according to procedure established by law' the words 'No person shall be deprived of his life or liberty without due process of law' be substituted."

The amendment was negated.

Vice-President: The question is:

"That in article 15, for the words 'except according to procedure established by law' the words 'due process of law' be substituted."

The amendment was negated.

Vice-President: No. 528.

SV Krishnamurthy Rao: I do not persist.

The amendment was, by leave of the Assembly, withdrawn.

Mr Vice-President: No. 530.The question is:

"That in article 15, for the words 'procedure established by law' the words 'due process of law' are substituted."

The amendment was negatived.

Vice-President: No. 527.The question is:

"That in article 15, for the words 'except according to procedure established by law' the words 'except in accordance with law' be substituted."

The amendment was negatived.

Mr Vice-President: I shall put the article to vote.

The question is:

That article 15 stand part of the Constitution.

The motion was adopted.

Article 15 was added to the Constitution.

OBSERVATIONS AND CONCLUSIONS

Assigning the job to prepare as important a document as the Constitution of a newly-formed country to a panel that comprised members of the legislative assembly—beneficiaries of the parliamentary system of the time—was not a wise decision. There was an obvious conflict of interest. In hindsight, it is not surprising at all that the members of the Constituent Assembly overwhelmingly wanted the British Parliamentary system to be adopted and were not even willing to discuss the other options.

The Drafting Committee should have ideally been a body of constitutional experts drawn from the people available within the country and even in other countries. This should have been a body to provide analytical review and analysis of the advantages and disadvantages of the two tried-out models of democracies in the world to help the members of the Constituent Assembly determine what was suitable for India. The draft of the Constitution that was tabled is somehow seen as the outcome of BR Ambedkar's personal efforts. Some members expressed their unhappiness at the very outset on the ground that the draft exceeded the given brief, and also it did not leave much room to discuss the possibility of having an alternative form of government for the new republic.

Two very important amendments were tabled by the members but rejected by the Chairman of the Drafting Committee. These were: The proposal to have a Presidential form of government with separation of powers and the change of the process of election of the President of the Union.

It is evident that KT Shah and a few others were strongly in favour of having a Presidential form of government in view of their bitter experience with the Parliamentary system since the promulgation of the two acts passed by the British Parliament in 1919 and 1935. Shah elaborated on the list of expected problems if India were to copy the British system in entirety. He pleaded that we should not assume that we would be able to emulate the English discipline of adhering to conventions and practices that had been developed in that country over a period of 700 years. He also pointed out that we were a much larger country with a lot more cultural and religious diversity which made it necessary to protect our minorities; and this could best be achieved through separation of powers in the Presidential form of Government. The proposal was rejected by the Chairman primarily on the grounds that some students of politics had criticised the system which separates the powers of the Executive and Legislature.

One expected that the proposal would be discussed for merits and demerits to help arrive at the best form of government for India. If it was felt that Presidential form of Government also had shortcomings, a debate should have been held on the possible ways of removing those shortcomings. Nothing of the sort happened. Just because there are some critics of a system, it does not make the system unworthy of emulating. All systems of governance are subjected to criticism; this has to be taken positively, as it is this criticism that helps to initiate a review process which, in turn, throws up possibilities of improvements and improvisations. Having worked with the British Parliamentary system for over 70 years without having succeeded in implementing their conventions and practices (which they had evolved over 700 years), we have acquired inherent problems that have become insurmountable impediments in our evolution as a mature democracy. These are:

1. Criminalisation of politics is perceived as the biggest threat to our democracy. The number of criminals who seek mandate and even get elected keeps increasing with every election, and yet, no political party is willing to refuse them tickets to fight election because they are a huge source of funds. Political parties desperately try to compete with each other to win over these criminals and get them into their fold. Money and muscle power are the new electioneering normal and these criminals are blessed with both. It is ironical that even the Supreme Court has shown helplessness in this regard. It has issued some kind of an advisory for the political parties knowing fully well that it would not be adhered to. Criminals want to be legislators to get protection from the police. A criminal turned legislator is the death knell for Indian democracy. In case we had complete separation of power, we would not have had this problem.
2. All our investigating agencies at the central as well as the state levels, such as the police, CBI, ED (Enforcement Directorate), IB (Intelligence Bureau) etc. are perceived to work in concert with the governments in power. Anna Hazare, an activist, sat on fast until death to pressurise the Central government to reform the system to get all such agencies to become independent. He relented to give up his fast on the assurance given by the then Central Government to legislate what is called the Lokpal Bill. People were very happy with what Anna Hazare had achieved and were looking forward to the changes in the system. Although the Act was legislated,

respective governments ever since have been dithering on the implementation citing some reason or the other for not moving ahead. The legislated Lokpal Act called for governments losing control over the appointment of their chosen officers in these agencies. Governments do not wish to lose control to achieve premeditated and motivated results of investigations. The Act has now fallen by the wayside. If we had a Presidential form of government, impartiality would be built in into the system. Even Presidents in USA have had to face impeachment proceedings for anti-government activities they were suspected to have committed.

3. Buying of legislators and parliamentarians for the sake of acquiring or retaining power. The price that is paid to individuals or a group of people for crossing over without becoming ineligible under the Anti-Defection Law is linked to the perception of the scale of wealth creation of the party if it remains in power. In the Presidential form, there is no possibility of this happening. The way legislators in India are seen behaving vis-a-vis their political masters is nothing short of 'political slavery'.
4. Parliamentarians and legislators are always ready to amend/modify business rules with the help of the executive to help businessmen in exchange for funds for the party or themselves. Earlier such transactions were done only in cash. Now, under the Electoral Bond Scheme introduced in 2018, a method has been improvised to accept donations legally by cheque without the information being made public. Clearly

there is a quid pro quo, as otherwise the directors of the companies would not allow the donations to be made. Such acts obviously require legislators to work in concert with the executive, which is not possible with the separation of powers. The Supreme Court—an institution that is normally a strong votary of transparency in public life—refused to amend the bill to make political donations transparent.

5. We are notorious for our excessive use of red tapism in the functioning of our bureaucracy. In the Presidential form of government, one does not have a common cadre manning different functions of the government. Presidents have the whole country to choose from to head the various functions of the government. The best brains can be hired for the jobs. The system does away with excessive red tapism in the working of the bureaucracy.
6. India has suffered incalculable loss for having been deprived of using the best brains and talent available in the country to head the various departments of the government. Our Parliamentary system makes it mandatory to select ministers from among the parliamentarians/legislators to man the ministries. This makes the choice extremely limited. Every fifth parliamentarian/legislator becomes a minister or a minister of state. If there is one reason why China has advanced so fast compared to us it is this. They have always employed highly educated and competent people for the jobs. Their growth story speaks for itself. To say that we are a democracy and should not be compared with China does not hold water. It is the

> English Parliamentary system that we have copied, without their conventions and practices, that needs to be blamed. We would have done equally well, perhaps even better, if we had a Presidential form of government.

In the debates of the Constituent Assembly, the second amendment tabled by KT Shah wanted the election of the President of India through adult citizens of the country, instead of through an electoral college comprising of elected members of the Parliament and State Legislatures. This amendment was supported by a number of other members who spoke on the subject arguing to have a President who is a sovereign, able to speak on behalf of all the people of India. They argued that if elected through an electoral college, the President would not be sovereign. He would, in that case, speak only on behalf of people who had elected the party in power. It is surprising that no one pointed out that the President has to be independent and sovereign if Judiciary has to be independent, as it is the President who signs on the warrants of appointment of the judges of the Supreme Court as well as the High Courts. It is inconceivable that the President, who is elected to the position by the party in power, would be able to exercise his authority to refuse approving the appointment of a judge recommended by a collegium through the party in power. The Constituent Assembly on putting the amendment to vote negated the motion. The reason given by the Chairman of the Drafting Committee and supported by a majority has been discussed in detail earlier. By this action, the independence of the Judiciary as also the governance of states has been seriously compromised.

There are a lot of shortcomings in the delivery of justice in our judicial system, not attributable to the Judiciary alone. Judiciary and executive in our country are interwoven in many areas. Sufficient resources, for example, are not provided by the State to relieve the judges of their workload. Judicial independence does not only mean the independence of judges from the interference of the executive. It requires independence in other aspects as well, and that independence has to be provided and facilitated by the State. It is the duty of the State to see that Judiciary is not overburdened without their having matching resources. And if that is absent, the Judiciary cannot be viewed as being independent.

If we were to endorse the proverbial adage 'justice delayed is justice denied', all that can be said is that the Indian justice delivery system has completely collapsed. With millions of cases pending in courts and judgments declared after the litigants are dead, the inefficiency in the system is institutionalised and the malaise deep-rooted.

The Supreme Court is seen as becoming ineffective over the execution of its own orders/directives. It is not able to get governments in States and the Centre to enforce its directives or judgments. Various judgments on water-sharing disputes between the States have not been implemented. In another case, seven directives issued to States and the Central government by the Supreme Court to depoliticise the police force and to separate the work of investigation of criminal cases from law and order have not been implemented. These directives were issued in 2006 for immediate implementation.

The Lokpal Bill was legislated many years ago and was meant to give independence to investigating agencies like CBI,

ED, IB, etc. by appointing independent officers. This has not been operationalised.

Four Supreme Court Judges had gone public on the question of lack of transparency on the part of the then Chief Justice. One of the four was appointed the next Chief Justice. He continued with the old practice adopted by his predecessor of nominating judges on the benches without consulting other senior judges. Many important cases involving the Central government were heard by the benches chaired by him with other judges nominated by him personally. Post retirement, he has managed a membership of the Rajya Sabha.

Recently, our Supreme Court refused to take up urgent Habeas Corpus petitions under PSA (Public Security Act). The Court has come under a lot criticism from many quarters on this issue. People charged under the Act continue to be in confinement, seemingly unconstitutionally.

These are but a few examples. There are many acts of the Supreme Court which are beyond comprehension. No one has any doubt that our Supreme Court is very soft when it comes to dealing with the government, particularly the Central Government. Our Supreme Court's record has not been very glorious. During the Emergency, in a Habeas Corpus petition appeal to the Supreme Court, the country was let down by four of the five seniormost judges of the Court for upholding the country's Attorney General's argument that fundamental rights under the Constitution were not applicable during Emergency. Justice HR Khanna, the sole dissenter, despite being seniormost, was superseded for the Chief's job. Such is the state of independence of our Judiciary. It is now taken for granted that our states are not bound by the judgments/

directives pronounced by our apex court. Our apex court is also seen to be overlooking the commissions and omissions of governments. Take for example booking people (students and journalists) for sedition. This is done despite clear directives issued by the Supreme Court to use the Sedition Act very restrictively. This Act was enacted way back by the British to muzzle Indians.

In the changed situation, it should be applied only when absolutely necessary. Years of harassment is caused to such people even if one knows that they will be let off eventually. Recall our Attorney General's plea in the Supreme Court that states do not obey Central Government's directives and that the Centre cannot order the states to comply. He requested the Court to take up the matter of implementation of judgments or the directives directly with the states.

Why and how have we got into such a situation needs to be analysed? Normally one would have expected our President to hold responsibility for keeping the Judiciary completely independent of the Executive. All the Members (barring a few), including the Chairman of the Drafting Committee, proclaimed their commitment to keeping the Judiciary independent, and yet, they did not see the importance of having a sovereign President to ensure the cause of impartial justice. The President has become a man of the party in power, who is supposed to do nothing more than just sign the proposals sent to him for approval. The executive branch of our government holds all the reins over governance including, to some extent, Judiciary. It was indeed a very serious mistake to have a President who is nominated by a party and elected by the electoral college which is divided on party lines.

The weak position of our presidents has been used by most governments in power. Earlier, presidents, acting through governors of states were made use of to suspend legally elected state governments run by parties in opposition in the centre. This used to be a common occurrence in earlier days. That has now been made difficult by various provisions introduced by the Supreme Court. Now the president is used for appointment of Governors specially chosen by the central government on the basis of the distinct qualification of having the capability to harass and cause hurdles for state governments ruled by parties in opposition. We are all aware of a president having been used by the then prime minister to declare Emergency for the personal reason of retaining her job and for no internal security threat.

The question that haunts the common man is, 'why do we have a President'? There is a certain aura about the office of the President and a huge grandeur associated with the Rashtrapati Bhawan. But ironically, what we associate the President with is just something ceremonial: award distribution; hoisting the flag on Republic Day; hosting parties in Mughal Garden; meeting international dignitaries at Rashtrapati Bhawan; reading out speeches from a text given to him on the eve of the Republic Day and getting rakhi tied by children on Rakshabandhan, etc.

The need to have the best intellectuals and professionals involved with public policy; the massive clean-up that is required in politics especially against the background of the growing and deep-rooted criminalisation; the growing nexus between the politicians and police that has generated colossal insecurity about safety of life and assets; and the executive and political interference with the institution of justice dispensation has made it necessary to have an objective evaluation of the efficacy of the Parliamentary Democracy that we have adopted. It is time that a national level debate is initiated to look at the option of having a Presidential form of government—which should have been at least discussed in the Constituent Assembly more than seventy years back.

For the survival of India and its transformation into a healthy democracy, we need to be seriously evaluating the factors that have held us back. This process has to be serious and ongoing. Friedrich Nietzsche, the German philosopher, had said that, "The snake which cannot cast its skin has to die. As well the minds which are prevented from changing their opinions; they cease to be mind."

REFERENCES

Prologue

1. Kunal Majumdar, 'Where was Mahatma Gandhi on 15 August 1947 when India became independent?' *Catch News,* 14 February 2017.
2. 'Independence Day Celebrations 1947'. Nehru Memorial Museum and Library, www.artsandculture.google.com
3. 'India's Tryst with Destiny', *In Focus,* www.inc.in
4. 'Great speeches of the 20th century', *The Guardian,* 8 February 2008.

Legacy of Poverty

1-2. 'Stanford scholar explains the history of India's partition, its ongoing effects today', *Stanford News,* 8 March 2019.

3. 'Living in the British empire–India', www.nationalarchives.gov.uk
4. Ashok Gulati, 'From plate to plough: Saluting our farmers', *Financial Express,* www.financialexpress.com

5 Shohini Bose, '26 Facts You Didn't Know About

the Indian Constitution', www.bloombergquint.com

6. 'India Population Live', www.worldmeter.info
7. 'List of States in India by Past Population' www.en.wikipedia.org (Calculated on the basis of 1951 Census Data)
8-9. 'Rangarajan defends poverty estimates', *The Hindu*, 21 October 2008.
10. 'Rs 27 per day: India's new rural poverty line'. www.downtoearth.org
11. Yogima Seth Sharma, "India has 100 million more poor: Rangarajan Committee', *Economic Times E Paper,* 7 July 2007.
12. 'World Poverty Clock by World Data Labs', www.worldpoverty.io
13 'Child Labour in India', www.soschildrensvillages.ca
14-15. 'Over 4 lakh beggars in India, WB tops chart', *Business Standard,* 21 March 2018.
16-18. 'Estimates Developed by the UN Inter-Agency Group for Child Mortality Estimation (UNICEF, WHO, World Bank, UN DESA Population Division)', www.childmortality.org
19-20. 'The Top 20 Economies in the World- Ranking the Richest Countries in the World', www.investopedia.org
21. 'Estimates Developed by the UN Inter-Agency Group for Child Mortality Estimation (UNICEF, WHO, World Bank, UN DESA Population Division)', www.childmortality.org
22. '68% of under-5 mortality in India still due to

malnutrition: Study', 20 September 2019, www.firstpost.com

23. 'Estimates Developed by the UN Inter-Agency Group for Child Mortality Estimation (UNICEF, WHO, World Bank, UN DESA Population Division)', www.childmortality.org
24. PB Jayakumar, 'Healthcare allocation in Budget 2020 5.7% lower than last budget', *Business Today,* 1 February 2020.
25. '30% of India is poor, says Rangarajan Panels new poverty line formula', *Poverty in India*, www.wikipedia.org
26. '10 facts–Poverty in India', www.borgenproject.org
27. 'Number and Population Below Poverty Line', *Reserve Bank of India,* www.wikipedia.org
28. Vikas Mohan, 'Agricultural Wastage is India's problem No 1. Here's Why'? *Times of India*, 4 September 2019. www.timesofinidia.indiatimes.com
29. 'Distribution of average monthly income in households across urban India in 2015', www.statistica.com
30. 'Unorganised Labour Force in India', www.vikaspedia.in
31. 'Labour in India', www.wikipedia.org
32. Shradul S Shroff, 'Labour and Employment Deskbook', Lex Mundi Publicatrions
33. 'Great Employment Transformation in China', www.ilo.org
34. Suneera Tandon, 'India's stunning economic

growth is hiding a staggering job crisis', *Quartz India,* 26 September 2018. www.qz.com

35. 'Demand for Jobs under MGNREGA in 2018-19 Was Highest in Eight Years', *The Wire,* 26 March 2019, www.thewire.in
36. '52.02 days of employment generated under MGNREGA: CAG report', *Financial Express,* 5 September 2018. www.thefinancialexpress.com
37. 'Analysis of Payment Delays and Delay Compensation in MGNREGA: Findings Across Ten States for Financial Year 2016–2017', *IDEAS,* www.ideas.repec.org
38. 'Union Budget 2020-21', www.indiabudget.gov.in
39. 'South West Monsoon Season', www.imdcennai.gov.in
40. Binayak Das, 'India's water Resources: Availability, usage and problems', www.base.d-p-h.info
41. 'National Perspective for Water Resource Development', *National Water Development Agency,* www.nwda.gov.in
42. 'Inland Water Transport Key to Reducing India's Logistics Cost', *CT Today,* www.constructiontechnology.in
43. 'Jawaharlal Nehru's address as Congress President (29 December 1929)', *A History of India,* www.cw.routledge.com
44. 'Annual Update of the HHS Poverty Guidelines', *Federal Register,* January 2020 www.federalregister.gov
45. 'India Unemployment Rate', *Trading Economics,*

www.tradingeconomics.com
46. 'India Labor Force Participation Rate', *Trading Economics*, www.tradingeconomics.com
47. 'Labor force participation rate, China', The World Bank, www.data.worldbank.org
48-49. 'GDP per capita (current US$)—China, India', T*he World Bank*, www.data.worldbank.org
50. Roshan Kishore, 'What's the average number of employees at a workplace in India?' *The Mint,* 9 April 2016, www.livemint.com
51. Bill Waddell, 'Productivity Rules', *Kevin Meyer*, www.kevinmeyer.com
52. 'Average yearly wages in the manufacturing sector in China', www.statistica.com
53. 'Average Production Worker Salary in India', www.paysscale.com
54. 'China's economic development in 40 years', www.chinadaily.com
55. 'Performances of Foreign Trade Sector in India', www.economicsdiscussion.net
56. Javier Silva-Ruete, 'The Development of China's Export Performance, 7 March 2006, www.imf.org
57. 'India's exports dip sharply in March; 2014-15 target missed' 17 April 2015, www.rediff.com
58. 'India's exports up 4% to 312.35 bn in 213-14', *PTI,* 11 April 2014 www.redifff.com
59. 'Exports rise 9.78% in 2017-18…' *PTI,* 13 April 2018, www.redifff.com
60. 'MSMEs to contribute 50% to India's GDP, provide 15 cr jobs in 5 years: Gadkari', *PTI,* 5 July

2019 www.economictimes.indiatimes.com

61 'Micro, Small, and Medium Enterprises in India – An Explainer', *India Briefing,* 14 May 2020, www.India-briefing.com

62-63. 'Micro, Medium & Small Scale Industry', www.cii.in

64. 'Economic Survey 2016-17', www.indiabudget.gov.in

65. 'Credit growth in MSME segment faces severe contraction…', www.rclipse.com

66. 'Micro, Medium & Small Scale Industry', www.cii.in

67. 'Italy: contribution of SMEs to the increase in GDP 2009-2017, by company size', 4 July 2019, www.statista.com

68. 'Number of SMEs in China 2012-2020', www.statista.com

69-70. 'India at a glance', *FAO in India*, www.fao.org

71. 'An overview of bovine breeding sector in India' *Department of Animal Husbandry and Dairying,* www.dahd.nic.in

72. 'What is the Sector-wise contribution of GDP in India?' www.jagranjosh.com

73. 'Government notifies extension of PM-KISAN scheme to all farmers', *Economic Times*, 8 June 2019, www.economictimes.com

74. Rahul Tongia, 'India's Biggest Challenge—The Future of Farming', 4 October 2019, www.theindianforum.in

75-78. 'Child Labor in India', *ILO,* www.ilo.org

79. 'Child Labour in India', www.wikipedia.org
80. 'Almost half a million Indian children produce cottonseed', www.stopchildlabour.org
81. Sriharsha Devulapalli, Vishnu Padmanabhan, 'India's police force among the world's weakest', *Mint*, 19 June 2019, www.livemint.com
82. '5.28 Lakh Posts Vacant in Police Forces; 1.29 Lakh in UP, 50,000 in Bihar', *NDTV*, 7 July 2019, www.ndtv.com
83. 'WTTC Annual Report: Key Highlights', www.wttc.org
84. 'India -Visitor Exports as a Share of Exports', *www.knoema.com*
85. 'India—Tourism Statistics 2019', www.blinkvisa.com

86-88. 'International Tourism Highlights 2019', www.e-unwto.org
89. 'India: Extreme Inequality in Numbers', *OXFAM International*, www.oxfam.org
90. Rukmini S 'India's workforce is masculinizing rapidly', *Mint*, 10 June 2019, www.lovemint.com
91. 'India: employment in agriculture' www.tradingeconomics.com
92. 'Economic Survey 2019-20', www.indiabudget.gov.in
93. 'GDP growth rate for 2017-18 revised upwards to 7.2%', www.conomictimes.indiatimes.com
94. 'Richest 1% cornered 73% Wealth Generated in India in 2017, *OXFAM Survey, 22* January 2018,

www.thewire.com

95. 'ILO: Global Wage Report', www.ilo.org
96. 'Extreme Inequality in Numbers', *OXFAM International,* www.oxfam.org
97. '*Union Budget of India 2018-19.Highlights of the Budget*'
98. *Wealth of India's Richest Soars on Forbes List., www.forbes.com*
99. 'China lifting 800 million people out of poverty is historic: World Bank', *PTI,* 13 *October 2017,* www.business-standard.com

Indian Police Under Captivity

1. 'The Gore Committee on Police Training', Ministry of Home Affairs, www.police.py.gov.in
2. 'Some Selected Recommendations of National Police Commission', www.humanrightsinitiative.org
3. 'Indian Police Service', www.wikipedia.org
4. 'Supreme Court of India: Prakash Singh and Ors vs Union of India and Ors – Judgement', 22 September 2006, www.indiankanoon.org

Waiting for Justice–Interminably

1. 'Indian Legal System – History, Development and Structure', www.shodhganga.inflibnet.ac.in
2. 'Courts and Justice System', blog.ipleaders.in
3. 'Introduction-Powers and Functions of the Supreme Court', www.blocles4u.com
4. 'Supreme Court gets four new judges; strength

reaches 34', *Economic Times,* 18 September 2019.

5. 'E-Courts Mission Mode Project', www.districts.ecourts.gov.in
6. 'Gram Nyayalayas', www.insightsonindia.com
7. 'Over 5,000 Gram Nyayalayas to be set up: Law Minister', *The Hindu,* 9 February 2011, www.thehindu.com
8. 'It'll take 320 years to clear legal backlog', *The Times of India*, 7 March 2010, www.timesofindia.indiatimes.com
9. Pradeep Thakur, 'Over 5000 vacancies in district and subordinate courts', *The Times of India*, 12 Dec 2018, www.timesofindia.indiatimes.com
10. 'Vital Stats', *PRS legislative Research*, www.prsindia.org
11. 'The Problem of Pending Cases in Indian Courts: How to tackle?' www.clearias.com

12-14. 'National Judicial Data Grid: Pending Dashboard', www.njdg.ecourts.gov.in

15. 'Over 1,000 cases pending in courts for 50 years: Chief Justice Ranjan Gogoi', *Business Line,* 4 August 2019, www.thehindubusinessline.com

16-17. 'Prison Statistics India', *National Crime Records Bureau,* www.ncrb.gov.in

18. 'Who is Nambi Narayanan?' *FE Online,* 14 September 2018, www.financialexpress.com
19. '1987 espionage case: Court acquits retired govt officer', *The News Scroll,* 7 February 2018, www.outlookindia.com
20. Harish Narasappa, 'Court Vacations–Are They

Justified?' *Bloomberg Quint Opinion,* 27 Dec 2018, www.bloomgerg.com

21. Roshni Sinha, 'Examining the Pendency of Cases in the Judiciary', *PRS Legislative Research*, www.prsindia.org

Diminishing Democracy

1. Rakesh Goyal, 'Democracy in Ancient India', *Pragyata,* 3 January 2017, www.prgyata.com
2. 'India slips 10 spots to 51st rank in annual Democracy Index due to erosion of civil liberties', 22 January 2020, www.scroll.in

3-4. 'Athenian Democracy', www.wikipedia.org

5. 'Magna Carta', www.wikipedia.org
6. 'Boston Tea Party', www.wikipedia.org
7. 'Battles of Lexington and Concord', www.wikipedia.org
8. 'Siege of Yorktown', www.wikipedia.org
9. 'Treaty of Paris', www.wikipedia.org
10. 'Government of India Act (1919 and 1935)', www.wikipedia.org

ABOUT THE AUTHOR

BR Taneja is the founder Managing Director of ISMT Limited, a Pune based steel/engineering conglomerate. He is a first generation entrepreneur and had a long innings with Tatas before he set out on his own in late 1970s. Within the corporate community he is considered to be a passionate technocrat, value driven manager, and an engaging mentor. His intellectual and academic interests are poverty and public policy. He is, along with his co-author, working on his next book which is a critical commentary on 'noble professions'.

Rakesh Duda has been working with ISMT Limited for the last two decades. He has earlier worked with Hero Group, USAID and NCAER. He is an engineer by training, a strategic planner and a people development manager by profession, a humanist by conviction and an academic floater and explorer by temperament.